a short & happy guide to Financial Well-Being

by

Sherri Burr
Regents Professor of Law
University of New Mexico School of Law

WEST ACADEMIC PUBLISHING

Mat #41625738

444 Cedar Street, Suite 700
St. Paul, MN 55101
1-877-888-1330

Printed in the United States of America

ISBN: 978-1-62810-039-6

This book is dedicated to my great-aunt Callie, great-great-aunts Lillian and Sill, and great-grandmother Zellar. Thank you for demonstrating the power of passive income and the advantage of managing money appropriately.

Acknowledgments

The author thanks the following individuals for reading various chapters of this book and providing feedback: Judith Schiess Avila, Sue Brown, Cheryl Burbank, Omar Durant, Penny Durant, Melody Groves, Lana Harrigan, Kathleen Hessler, Phil Jackson, Sue Mann, Nathalie Martin, Paula Paul, Pat Sutton, Kelly Williams, Carolyn Wheelock, and Patricia Woody.

She is also grateful to the following individuals at West Academic for their enthusiastic support of this book: James Cahoy, Staci Herr, Louis Higgins, Robb Westawker, Greg Olson, Pam Siege Chandler, and Laura Holle.

In conclusion, the author appreciates the many individuals, including the named and the anonymous, who shared stories or were interviewed for this book.

Table of Contents

A Short & Happy Guide to Financial Well-Being

Introduction

During the current recession, which began around December 2007, the U.S. economy lost over 15,000 legal jobs and 250,000 public education positions, and downgraded numerous other employments. As access to credit tightened, some individuals lost the ability to borrow for cars, homes and other items. Even as undergraduate and professional students found loans to finance their education, interest rates rose. This situation necessitates educating law students, lawyers, judges, secretaries, teachers and the general public to mind their finances.

A Short & Happy Guide to Financial Well-Being is a money management manual for individuals seeking education so they can thrive in both weak and healthy economic times. It provides advice on eliminating debt, spending frugally, managing credit, purchasing cars and homes, saving money, writing wills, adjusting to downsizing, and filing for bankruptcy. The book is set up in a tip format, offering advice in an easy to follow fashion for individuals like law and medical students seeking to manage their personal finances while in school, and will serve them well when their finances improve upon graduation and the obtaining of a job.

This book intersperses individual interviews, the author's personal experiences, and colorful characters like Dedicated Doctor, Joyful Judge, Lively Law Student, Learned Lawyer, Published Poet, Reliable Realtor, and Seattle Businessman to explain complex financial matters. Through these characters, *A Short & Happy Guide to Financial Well-Being* provides financial advice in an often humorous manner.

Certain characters like Learned Lawyer, Lively Law Student, Published Poet, and Scattered Secretary appear throughout the book. Published Poet, for example, is introduced in the first chapter as a person who adopts a phone code to dodge creditors, and readers will follow her through a number of problematic circumstances as she loses her home, and twice files for bankruptcy. Learned Lawyer appears in various chapters as a person who navigated requests from relatives for loans, and as a busy professional who adopted simplified investment strategies to avoid scams. Scattered Secretary demonstrates the advantages of eliminating debt, while Lively Law Student showcases how to spend frugally and search for the free or nearly free items and services.

The tips are practical. Those who mind their finances during difficult times will be situated to move forward into the economy's good times.

This book is grouped into four parts. Part I provides the basics to becoming financially literate. Part II offers savings and prudent investment tips. Part III delivers tips for the financially struggling, including those who have been downsized or gone bankrupt. Part IV conveys information helpful to all individuals seeking to improve their lives.

A Short & Happy Guide to Financial Well-Being is a gift of knowledge to you, your relatives and your friends. When it comes to managing money, ignorance is not bliss.

PART 1

Financial Literacy Basics

CHAPTER 1

Credit Dodger No More

The phone rang incessantly. Published Poet, a creative person in her seventies on Social Security, didn't dare answer. She feared the threats and name calling. Instead, Published Poet adopted a phone code and shared it only with her closest family members and friends. They were instructed to dial her number, let the phone ring once, hang up, and then dial again. She would answer the second time.

Why did Published Poet adopt a scheme before she would pick up her ringing telephone? To distinguish friend from foe, namely collection agencies harassing her at all hours. When the collection agencies eventually figured out the code, she disconnected her phone altogether so no one could reach her.

Scattered Secretary worked for a law firm and was organized at work, but disorganized at home. As his bills mounted, he put together a simple system to determine which ones to pay. He drew a line in a room with a belt or another item and then tossed the bills into the air. The bills that landed on the positive side got paid, the others got pitched into the circular file, otherwise known as the trash can.

In the lean years before his bestselling book *Act Like a Lady, Think Like a Man* made him exceedingly wealthy, comedian Steve Harvey developed a distinct method of curtailing phone calls from collection agents. When they rang asking him if he had a plan to pay his debts, he explained he put all the creditor names in the hat and drew out the bills to be paid that month. If particular agents continued to call, Harvey told them, I won't put your names in the hat.

With the national government running up trillions of dollars in debt, U.S. citizens are not far behind in piling up mountains of debt for homes, cars, student loans, credit cards and so forth. For example, Americans went from saving 7.5% of their income in 1991 to less than zero percent by 2006, meaning that they spent more than they earned. The last time the national savings rate went negative was during the Great Depression when jobs became scarce in a contracting economy with a 25% unemployment rate.

During a thriving 2006 economy, Americans like Published Poet and Scattered Secretary were borrowing to support their spending habits and finding themselves eventually overwhelmed by their debt and badgered by collection agencies. Published Poet went into therapy for compulsive shopping in 2007 and filed for bankruptcy in 2008, a legal process for which she felt ashamed, particularly as it was her second time. In a deteriorating 2009 economy, many Americans borrowed to survive, while even more came to terms with prior financial excesses as their homes were foreclosed and they declared bankruptcy, attempting to save the last shreds of their American dream.

This chapter explores issues associated with managing debt. It counsels how to climb out of debt if you've arrived at the point where you need a phone code to keep the collection agencies at bay, or are running a debt lottery to determine which bills to pay. Above all, this chapter encourages acknowledging and accepting debt and taking concrete steps either to pay it off or seek relief by negotiating a reduction in monthly payments or filing for bankruptcy. As the legendary inventor, diplomat, printer and Founding Father Benjamin Franklin long ago said, "It is necessary for me to be extremely frugal for some time, till I have paid what I owe."[1]

Tip 1: Add Up the Debt

Most people open their mail as it arrives. In extreme cases, people like Published Poet and Scattered Secretary have been known to let envelopes stack up for years. This causes frustration for creditors if they cannot reach the person by mail, phone, email, text, social media, or other means. Pretending the bills don't exist by hurling them in the trash or stacking them in a corner doesn't help the problem. Rather, it only delays the inevitable and augments the damage. As interest charges and fees for late payments and non-payments get tacked on, the original debt doubles, triples and quadruples.

Some people may be tempted to follow Published Poet's and Scattered Secretary's examples and dodge their creditors by not answering their phones or opening their mail. Never do this. Open all envelopes as soon as they arrive. If you have a heap of un-opened mail, schedule an envelope opening session. Do this yourself or get someone you trust to help. You must participate.

At the appointed time, open all the envelopes and sort them by creditor name. At the top of a handwritten notepad or on a computer screen, write or type down the following categories: creditor name, total amount owed, minimum payment, and due date. If handwritten, draw lines down the pads to separate the

---

[1] Walter Isaacson, Benjamin Franklin: An American Life 49 (Simon & Schuster, NY: 2003), quoting The Autobiography of Benjamin Franklin 183.

categories. If on a computer, create tables in word processing or use a spreadsheet. After you have done either of these, write or type the information for every creditor. Do not skip any. Your columns should look something like those in Table 1-1 for Scattered Secretary:

Table 1-1: Scattered Secretary's Debt

Creditor Name	*Total Amount Owed*	*Minimum Payment*	*Due Date*
Charge Account #1	$237	$10	January 1
Visa Card #1	$5303	$110	January 21
MasterCard #1	$4702	$100	January 17
Catalog #1	$732	$20	January 4
Charge Account #2	$358	$10	January 22
Visa #2	$7398	$150	January 18
MasterCard #2	$2351	$50	January 9
Diner's Club	$9356	$190	January 20
Totals	*$30,437*	*$640*	

Take a calculator and figure out the total amount you owe, and the total minimum amount you owe. While the total may shock you, don't bother fainting. Breathe. You have to deal with the situation.

In the Table 1-1 scenario, Scattered Secretary owes $30,437, with minimum payments due of $640. This example assumes Scattered Secretary has paid on time and has not been charged late fees or non-payment fees. These fees can easily double the minimum due to $1180 or triple it to $1770.

When Published Poet charted her debt, she owed five times her yearly income and the minimum payments exceeded her monthly income. Even if she stopped paying her rent or buying food, she would not have been able to pay minimum amounts to her creditors. Her only option was bankruptcy. If your situation is similar, then you should skip to Chapter 9's discussion of the bankruptcy process. If your circumstances are not that dire, continue reading this chapter.

Tip 2: Pay Bills Before the Due Dates

Next, review the due dates. Take another sheet and list each debt in order of due date. The chart should look like Table 1-2 for Scattered Secretary:

Table 1-2: Scattered Secretary's Due Dates

Creditor	*Due Date*	*Minimum Amount Due*
Charge Account #1	January 1	$10
Catalog #1	January 4	$20
MasterCard #2	January 9	$50
MasterCard #1	January 17	$100
Visa #2	January 18	$150
Diner's Club	January 20	$190
Visa #1	January 21	$110
Charge Account #2	January 22	$10
Totals		$640

Figure out the minimum payments due by the time of your next paycheck. In this hypothetical example, Scattered Secretary gets paid twice a month on January 1 and January 15. He would need to pay a minimum of $80 after receiving his first paycheck and $560 following his second.

Do your best to put all minimum payments in the mail five days before their due date. This guarantees that if your payment is mailed in the midst of a holiday, it will still arrive on time. If you are struggling to pay by a particular due date, call the company and request to change the date to one more compatible with when you get paid or have other income coming in. For example, if you get paid once a month on the last day of the month, have your due dates set for the fifteenth of the month. If you have multiple due dates and want to simplify your bill paying, then try having them all changed to the same date.

Also explore paying online if this is more convenient. You save the price of postage stamps, and it increases the chances that you will meet your due dates. Most bills get paid by the second business day online. Even online, it can take up to five business days for the company to be paid. If a company does not take online payments, the bank cuts a check and mails it.

Part of your credit score, which is calculated by the Fair Isaac Corporation (FICO), is determined by timely payments. Even if you owe a lot of money, you can improve your FICO credit score just by paying on time.

Tip 3: Stop Borrowing to Support Your Lifestyle

Part of the challenge of staying out of debt is to stop borrowing money to maintain a certain lifestyle. Instead, adopt a cash-only lifestyle. Pay for groceries and other necessities with cash, check, or debit card. Cut up or shred all credit and charge cards, with the exception of one general credit card, like a Visa or MasterCard. You will need it for online airline, rental car, auction, and retail purchases. Vow never to charge anything on your one credit card that you cannot pay off in its entirety immediately.

If you cut up the credit cards and remove them from your wallet, you reduce temptation. Most importantly, however, do not close accounts that do not have annual fees if you wish to avoid a negative hit to your credit score. The Fair Isaac Corporation calculates your debt to available credit ratio in computing your final score. If you reduce your debt while keeping your available credit, your credit score will improve. Keeping accounts open requires financial discipline as you must continue to resist borrowing on these cards to pay for purchases.

Tip 4: Carefully Consider Borrowing to Invest in Education

If you are borrowing to invest in your education, like Lively Law Student, that is another matter. This can be smart borrowing if it leads to a good paying job. However, over-borrowing can lead to financial disaster.

In 2011, the New York Times profiled Michael Wallerstein who borrowed over $250,000 while attending Thomas Jefferson School of Law in San Diego, California.[2] Mr. Wallerstein, according to the Times, could not afford to pay down interest and thus watched the outstanding loan balance grow. He is, said the Times, "in roughly the same financial hell as people who bought more home than they could afford during the real estate boom. But creditors can't foreclose on him because he didn't spend the money on a house."

This is not the kind of situation any undergraduate or graduate student should want to create. Mr. Wallerstein would have been better off carefully monitoring the amount of money he was borrowing for his education and tracking available jobs. He

[2] David Segal, *Is Law School a Losing Game?*, N.Y. Times (Jan. 8, 2011).

should not have borrowed more money than an average job in his planned specialty would permit him to repay his debts.

According to the Times, Mr. Wallerstein "rented a spacious apartment. He also spent a month studying in the South of France and a month in Prague—all on borrowed money. There were cost-of-living loans, and tuition of about $33,000 a year. Later came a $15,000 loan to cover months of studying for the bar."

These expenses added up for Mr. Wallerstein, and are to be carefully considered if Lively Law Student does not wish to wind up with excessive debt he cannot repay. Discharging student debt in bankruptcy is exceedingly difficult. The standard under Federal bankruptcy law requires former students to prove to a judge that repaying it will cause an "undue hardship." As the New York Times reported, "one component of that test is often convincing a federal judge that there is a 'certainty of hopelessness' to their financial lives for much of the repayment period."[3]

Tip 5: Pay off Your Debt

Once you're in the habit of paying all bills on time, the next step is to engage in debt reduction. Paying the minimum rarely makes a dent in the principal, and the credit card companies like it that way. Indeed, they set the minimum low to encourage you to remain in debt. Do not fall into their traps. Resolve to pay off your debt.

There are two primary approaches to reducing debt. Some commentators argue you should pay off the debt with the highest interest first. Others advise paying off the lowest amount owed first. After listening to a series of tapes on "Debt Free Lifestyle," I successfully used the latter strategy to retire my debt. I

---

[3] Ron Lieber, *Last Plea on School Loans: Proving a Hopeless Future*, N.Y. Times (Aug. 31, 2012).

recommend this approach for the following reason: you see progress immediately, which encourages you to keep going.

In Table 1-3, Scattered Secretary pays off the debt in the order of least owed. Let's say he calculates he can contribute an additional $250 a month toward reducing his debt. He would pay the minimum on all the other cards and an additional $227 of the $250 for Charge Account #1 for a total of $237 (the $10 minimum plus the balance). This would leave him an additional $23 that he can apply to Charge Account #2, his second lowest balance. This month, he would pay $33 for Charge Account #2.

Table 1-3: Reducing Debt by Least Amount Owed

Creditor Name	*Total Owed*	*Minimum Payment*	*Extra Payment*
Charge Account #1	$237	$10	$227 ($237 total)
Charge Account #2	$358	$10	$23 ($33 total)
Catalog #1	$732	$20	
MasterCard #2	$2351	$50	
MasterCard #1	$4702	$100	
Visa Card #1	$5303	$110	
Visa #2	$7398	$150	
Diner's Club	$9356	$190	
Totals	*$30,437*	*$640*	

The next month, assuming Scattered Secretary has not charged more, he applies the minimum payment from Charge Account #1 of $10 to his debt reduction fund so it grows to $260. He then focuses on Charge Account #2, whose new balance, with additional interest, is $338. He pays the minimum of $10 plus his debt reduction fund of $260 to Charge Account #2, reducing its balance to $78.

Table 1-4: Reducing Debt—Month #2			
Creditor Name	*Total Owed*	*Minimum Payment*	*Extra Payment*
Charge Account #2	$338	$10	$260 ($270 total)

The following month, Scattered Secretary pays off Charge Account #2, which is down to $78 including interest. He then applies the remaining $192 of his debt reduction fund to Catalog #1.

Table 1-5: Reducing Debt—Month #3			
Creditor Name	*Total Owed*	*Minimum Payment*	*Extra Payment*
Charge Account #2	$78	$10	$68 ($78 total)
Catalog #1	$721	$20	$192 ($212 total)

Using this method, Scattered Secretary can pay off Catalog #1 in three months with the debt reduction fund that grew to $270 per month after Charge Account #2 was paid off. Within six months, he will have reduced his number of creditors from eight to five. He's on a roll. Five years later, Scattered Secretary will be debt free if he does not borrow any more money. This approach can also be used by Lively Law Student to pay student loans.

Tip 6: Balance Your Checkbook Monthly

A lawyer told me she and her lawyer husband did not record any written checks or debit purchases in their checkbook. Indeed, they never wrote anything down, not even their income. Two people writing checks on the same account with no recording seemed a recipe for disaster. As I looked at her in amazement, she said, “We have overdraft protection.” Her husband later added, “I used to record checks until I married her. After that it became too complicated.”

The woman wasn’t so prideful the year she and her husband underpaid their taxes by approximately $30,000 and had to raid savings accounts and liquidate financial products to pay the IRS. Their approach to checkbook registration signaled their approach to all their finances.

Don’t be like these two lawyers. Record all checks and debit purchases in your register and periodically balance your checkbook against your bank statement. This is particularly important if you are using debit cards to pay for daily purchases. The amount in your account can quickly evaporate if you are not recording it.

You can opt to subtract the amount spent immediately or, if you don’t feel competent about your math, calculate the numbers on your computer, tablet, phone or other smart device. Set up a system and strive to use it at least once a week, but no less than once a month. The most common computer program is Quicken, or you can create your own spreadsheets using Excel.

Table 1-6 presents a sample checkbook registration for Scattered Secretary, which reflects that his bi-monthly pay from his law firm job and outgoing expenditures. Notice the headings track those typically found in a checkbook register. AD stands for automatic deposit, AP for automatic payment, FT for funds transfer, and ATM for cash withdrawal.

Table 1-6: Scattered Secretary's Checkbook Registration						
TRANS. TYPE or CHECK NO	DATE	DESCRIPTION OF TRANSACTION	PAYMENT/ DEBIT	FEE	DEPOSIT/ CREDIT	BALANCE
AD	1/1	Salary Income			$2198.27	$2,198.27
FT	1/1	Transfer to Savings	$200			$1,998.27
ATM	1/1	Cash	$100			$1,898.27
AP	1/1	Bank (Mortgage)	$1334			$564.27
1005	1/1	Charge Account #1	$237			$327.27
1006	¼	Catalog #1	$20			$307.27
1007	1/9	MasterCard #2	$50			$257.27
AD	1/15	Salary Income			$2198.27	$2455.54
FT	1/15	Transfer to Savings	$200			$2255.54
ATM	1/15	Cash	$300			$1955.54
1008	1/16	Gas & Electric Company	$230.45			$1725.09
1009	1/16	Telephone Company	$78.98			$1646.11

1010	1/16	Cable & Internet	$95.37			$1550.74
1011	1/17	MasterCard #1	$100			$1450.74
1012	1/18	Visa #2	$150			$1300.74
1013	1/20	Diner's Club	$190			$1110.74
1014	1/21	Visa #1	$110			$1000.74
1015	1/22	Charge Account #2	$33			$967.74
ATM	1/25	Cash	$400			$567.74

No matter the program used for tracking, balancing your checkbook should keep you from spending more than you earn. Also it allows you to monitor your bank, because sometimes institutions make mistakes. By balancing your statement against bank receipts, you know exactly how much money you have in your checking account and whether you can afford to put more money into debt reduction, splurge on a new pair of shoes, or take a colleague to lunch to celebrate a promotion. You may have to settle instead for shopping consignment or resale stores for clothing and shoes, and bringing your colleague a congratulatory card. The bottom line should always be if you don't have the money, don't spend it. One grandmother asks herself, "Can I do without it?" This is a good question to pose before purchasing discretionary items.

Tip 7: Negotiate with Creditors

You can negotiate with your creditors. Usually, they are willing to reduce your debt in hopes of receiving some payment.

The phone numbers are available on credit card statements. Push the buttons that will transfer you to the operator. Ask for the person who will be in the best position to negotiate your debt. Explain your dilemma to the negotiator and say you would like them to reduce your debt by 75%.

They may offer another percentage reduction, and ask you to pay off the entire amount at once. This could be a good strategy if you have been laid off and received a considerable severance payment. Under these circumstances, you may want to reduce your debt quickly to decrease monthly outflow.

If you cannot pay it off at once, seek to lower overall debt. In most instances, companies will consider eliminating the fees and extra interest they have tacked on to your account. Thus, they are not losing money *per se*, but rather giving up the opportunity to make excess profits at your expense. In short, aim to have them at least reduce the debt they added to your account.

Further, if the bank tacks on other fees and increases your interest rate, call them to complain. After Congress passed a law in May 2009 to limit their ability to raise interest rates and tack on additional fees, several banks started doing so before the law went into effect in February 2010. Even consumers who had never missed a payment found their interest rates doubled. One tactic that works for consumers in good standing is to say, "You can remove the fee (or lower the interest rate) or you can close this account: what's it going to be?" If the person says they cannot do anything, ask to speak to someone who can. It's your money. Don't give it to a bank or lending institution if you don't have to.

Tip 8: Obtain Your Annual Credit Reports and FICO Score

To obtain your annual credit reports, call 1-877-322-8228 or go to the website www.annualcreditreport.com. This site was set up by the three major credit reporting agencies to simplify the process. Be prepared to provide the following information: name (and previous names if you have recently changed a name for marriage or other reason), social security number, date of birth, current employer and address, and home address and previous addresses.

You can also contact the three major credit reporting companies directly:

EQUIFAX
Credit Report Request
P.O. Box 105281
Atlanta, GA 30348-5281
Automatic Ordering Center: 1-800-685-1111
Fraud Assistance Service Center: 1-800-525-6285

EXPERIAN
Credit Report Request
475 Anton Boulevard
Costa Mesa, CA 92626
1-888-397-3742; 1-800-831-5614

TRANSUNION
Consumer Disclosure Center
P.O. Box 1000,
Chester, PA 19022
Credit Report Request: 1-877-322-8228
Fraud Victim Assistance Division: 1-800-680-7289
Credit Disputes: 1-800-916-8800

If you chose to write, here's a sample letter in Table 1-7. Send the letters separately.

Table 1-7: Sample Letter to Request Free Annual Credit Report

Name

Address ♦ City, State, Zip Code

Phone Number ♦ Email Address

Date

EQUIFAX
Credit Report Request
P.O. Box 105281
Atlanta, GA 30348-5281

Dear Sir/Madam:

I write to request my annual complimentary credit report. The information you need is as follows:

Name (and Previous Names if relevant):

Current and previous addresses:

SSN:

DOB:

Current Employer & Address:

Office Phone:

Thank you.

Sincerely,

Name

All individuals are entitled to a free report from each of these agencies every year. You can obtain additional free reports after being denied credit. Some people order all three at once, but consider spacing them out and ordering a different one every fourth month. This permits you to monitor your credit progress. Be wary of www.freecreditreport.com. This is a private service owned by Experian, and it ropes people into signing up for services that cost monthly fees. By sticking to the official website www.annualcreditreport.com, you do not have to pay.

To obtain your actual credit score, go to www.myfico.com and order it there, either directly or sign up for a free 30-day trial that alerts you when your credit score changes. If you do not wish to pay monthly charges, flag your personal organizer to remind you to cancel once the complimentary period has expired. You may wish to keep the trial going if you have experienced problems with identity theft and need to continuously monitor attempts to open credit in your name.

Credit scores range from 300 to 850. A score above 760 is most desirable as it signals superb credit, eligible for the best mortgage rates. In forty states, some businesses can require potential employees who will be handling money and financial resources to reveal their credit scores before offering them a job. Employers think this separates out weaker employees on the theory that if they cannot manage their finances, they will probably be unreliable. This is potentially problematic as it can make it more difficult for those who most need a job to acquire one. Just be alert that this issue could come up as part of a job application.

In ten states (California, Colorado, Connecticut, Hawaii, Illinois, Maryland, Nevada, Oregon, Vermont, and Washington), however, businesses are barred from requiring applicants to share their credit histories. On December 17, 2013, Senator Elizabeth

Warren submitted a proposed bill to amend the Fair Credit Reporting Act, § 1837, to extend this ban nationwide. Warren believes that "poor credit ratings say more about how hard a time people who want to work have had in recent years than about a person's character." [See http://thinkprogress.org/economy/2013/12/17/3076681/elizabeth-warren-ban-credit-checks-hiring/]

Furthermore, insurance companies also check credit scores. They offer their best rates for housing, car, and other insurance to those with excellent credit scores on the theory that those who manage their finances are less likely to demand an insurance payout.

Tip 9: Immediately Order a Credit Report or Cancel a Card If Notified of a Security Breach

In December 2013, Target posted a notification on its website that "unauthorized access may impact guests who made credit or debit card purchases in our U.S. stores from Nov. 27 to Dec. 15, 2013." In other words, the Target security system was hacked during the busiest shopping season of the year. Target estimated the cyber thieves obtained over 40 million customer names, credit and debit card numbers, and the card's expiration date and CVV, or Card Verification Value. This is a three to four numeric code on the front of the card that differs from the three-digit security code on the back of the card. Target said the security codes were not impacted.

Target recommended customers request a credit report from Equifax, Experian and TransUnion, and provided additional information for those who become victims of an identity theft. What happened at Target, a store that spends millions of dollars a year on security, exemplifies why individuals should consider shopping with cash, a topic to be further discussed in Chapter 3 on Spend Frugally.

For those consumers who did not want to constantly monitor their cards for potential theft had the additional option to cancel cards and request new ones. Although some banks indemnify (hold individuals harmless) against all losses, it can be tricky to track the small purchases that thieves charge to test the validity of the card. A charge of $2.25 or $25.20 could easily escape notice and someone might pay the inappropriate amount. For individuals who seek peace of mind, it's easier to just obtain a new credit card with a new number.

Tip 10: Get Help If Necessary

If you are one of the millions of Americans who have become overwhelmed with debt, then it may be wise to seek help through Debtors Anonymous or credit counseling services. To find a group meeting near you, visit the website www.debtorsanonymous.org, write to Debtors Anonymous General Service Office at P.O. Box 920888, Needham, MA 02492, or call 1-800-421-2383.

Some people explore credit counseling services. Unfortunately many of these take people's money without reducing or paying their debt. This has created a fraudulent reputation for an entire industry. Before hiring one of these services, investigate the reputation of the company by contacting the Better Business Bureau in your area.

You can also get individual attention by seeing a psychologist paid from your own pocket or by your medical insurance.

Tip 11: Embrace the Debt-Free Lifestyle

Advantages accrue to debt-free individuals. They have higher credit scores. They have more money to spend on the items they value. They also have less stress because they do not worry about being harassed by creditors. Nor do they fear opening envelopes containing bills.

To be debt free brings empowerment. You are less likely to be affected by the vagaries of our economic system. You can survive economic downturns without losing sleep. If you are downsized, you can adjust to the sudden turn in your economic fortunes. Even if you win the lottery, being debt free helps you adjust to sudden windfalls. Unfortunately, over 95% of lottery winners end up in worse financial shape five years after winning the lottery. If you are debt free before the addition to your wealth, you will most likely remain debt free after.

By determining to become debt free, your credit dodging days cease to exist. Answer the phone without hesitation, knowing that a collection agent is not on the line. Open all envelopes containing bills, confident that you have the funds to pay them. Overall, your life will become more enjoyable.

CHAPTER 2

Nor a Lender Be

"Neither a borrower nor a lender be" is a phrase from Shakespeare's Hamlet Act 1, Scene 3, that provides helpful guidance to mind your finances, reduce your stress, and increase your happiness. In *Chapter 1: Credit Dodger No More*, we discussed problems arising from excessive borrowing and how to seek freedom from the ravages of debt. This Chapter focuses on the second part of the phrase's wisdom, which Learned Lawyer had to learn the hard way. Lending money to relatives and friends can have disastrous consequences on an individual's financial solvency.

Early in her adult life, Learned Lawyer repeatedly loaned money to relatives, particularly her siblings. Not one of them ever repaid a single dollar. Learned Lawyer became so frustrated trying to collect that she finally just forgave the bad debts. After doing this for over a decade, she realized she was practicing what someone long ago described as insanity: always doing the same thing while expecting a different result. The loans diminished her trust in the borrowers and caused her to resent them. This brings us to the first tip of this chapter.

Tip 1: Do Not Destroy Relationships by Loaning Money

Consider this story from a Seattle Businessman, a person I first met at a conference in Phoenix in 2008. After I set down at his table for breakfast, Seattle Businessman told this story. He had received a call from one of his friends who said, "I'm in deep sh-t! The mob is after me. I gambled and lost four thousand dollars. If I don't pay by tomorrow evening, they're going to kill me. Can you loan me the cash?"

When Seattle Businessman received this call, he had just caught his wife cheating on him. He said to me, "I decided to loan him the money because if he paid me back, it would restore my faith in humanity."

"You were counting on a compulsive gambler being chased by the mob to restore your faith in humanity?" I asked, incredulously.

"Yes," Seattle Businessman said. "If I saved his life and he paid me back, there would be proof that there is a God."

"So what did you do?"

"I went to my freezer and I took out four thousand dollars and deposited it in his bank account the next day," he responded with a slight stutter.

"You keep money in the freezer? Did you have to thaw it overnight?"

"No. Money doesn't freeze."

"Why keep it in the freezer?"

"Because that is the last place a burglar would look, and I need an emergency stash in case something happens and I have to leave quickly."

"Like what kind of emergency?"

"An earthquake. A lot of people don't know that Seattle sits on an earthquake fault line."

"Oh. So what happened? Did he pay you back?"

"He called a couple of weeks later and asked if he could borrow three thousand more. He said his wife left him and he had an urgent need to hire a private investigator."

"Did you loan him the money?" I asked.

"Yes. I took another three thousand from the freezer and deposited it in his bank account. He said he'd pay me back in three weeks."

"Did he?"

"I got back seven hundred. He actually lives in Arizona now. He wrote me recently to say that he's in Gamblers Anonymous and he wants to make amends by paying back a little every week. I haven't seen a dime."

"How much money do you have left in the freezer?" I asked, my mind fixated on the cold cash.

"About four thousand."

"Wow," I said. It occurred to me that this was a story he could only tell a stranger.

Seattle Businessman went on to tell me about how he had also loaned money to two employees, one in danger of losing his car and the other behind on his mortgage payments. The businessman said he thought it would motivate them to sell more and become loyal employees. One of them left anyway.

The story of this businessman illustrates how borrowed money can destroy relationships, be they friendships or that of employer/employee. He came to almost hate the men who borrowed from him. He got so upset just talking about the loaned money that his stutter became more pronounced. I suggested that he let the debts go and call them gifts. "You'll get more money from other sources," I told him.

He wouldn't hear of it. As his stutter became more pronounced, he insisted he could collect money from the men who owed him. There is a 99.99% chance that he will never be repaid in full. Is it worth a stutter becoming more pronounced to hold on to a 0.01% chance that someone might pay you back?

The reality, however, is that his chances of collection had been killed when the loans sent his relationships to the graveyard of friendship. Next time friends or family members ask to borrow money recall the phrase, "A fool and his money are soon parted." Don't play the fool. Become financially literate. Tell them you value their companionship too much to endanger it by tainting it with money. You'll be less stressed when you don't have to worry about being repaid, and happy that you kept your money.

Tip 2: Ignore the Excuse and Its Urgency

Reliable Realtor befriended a foreign widow who was left with no assets when her husband died suddenly. The deceased had three children from a previous marriage and left his estate to them. Reliable Realtor's husband, a friend of the deceased, asked her to look after the widow. One day the widow called Reliable Realtor from Los Angeles. The widow said a furniture store was having a fire sale and requested that Reliable Realtor wire $50,000 through Western Union within three hours so the widow could buy the furniture and resell it quickly for a profit to someone she knew. With the proceeds, she could take care of herself, the widow assured Reliable Realtor. Moved by the urgency of the request, Reliable Realtor wired the money from her bank account to the foreign widow.

Did the widow return the money? No. Instead, as in the case with Seattle Businessman, she asked for more with a different story. Reliable Realtor gave it to her, wiping out her bank account.

Reliable Realtor had remembered her husband mentioning the widow's propensity to bet in Las Vegas. But ignorant of such matters, Reliable Realtor did not immediately connect the request with gambling. People like the widow come up with excuse after excuse as to why they need *your* money and they sound desperate to limit *your* time to respond. If you get such a request, take time out. Breathe. Then kindly say "no" and hang up the phone, quickly.

When I repeated this story to groups, there was often a great deal of empathy expressed for Reliable Realtor. One person blurted out, "I loaned ten thousand dollars to two separate friends and they fixed me. They both died of cancer before repaying me."

In kindly agreeing to let me share her story, Reliable Realtor said, "There are so many of the gullibles and the predators."

Don't become one of them. You will feel shame that you have been duped. When someone comes forth with a dire plea for *your* money, stop the conversation. Ignore the urgency.

Tip 3: Disregard Attempts to Associate Loans with Love

Relatives may attempt to link their request to borrow money with your love for them. "If you loved me, you'd loan me the money" is a common plea of this sort. One relative asked Learned Lawyer to loan him $1000 so that he could upgrade the casket for his father. The difference between the $1595 casket and the $2595 casket was that the latter had more steel and moveable handles. When Learned Lawyer suggested his relative stick to the budget set by his father's insurance policy, the relative raged about burying their father in "a cheap-ass casket."

The relative's shouts implied that if Learned Lawyer loved him and his father, she would pay an additional $1000 to upgrade his father's casket. While Learned Lawyer loved him, she did not relish the thought of burying money into the ground, literally. This relative owed $1000 to his cell phone company, which had cut off his business cell phone, and thus Learned Lawyer knew her relative could never repay the $1000.

These can be difficult situations to defuse, but the important thing to remember is Hamlet's plea, "To thine own self be true." When someone attempts to associate loans with love, they are creating a lose/lose situation for all concerned. There can never be enough money to provide the love they seek, and thus they will always feel deprived of your affection no matter how much of your hard earned cash you fork over.

Tip 4: Turn the Tables

Learned Lawyer also had an aunt who went through a gambling phase. The aunt would frequently call family members seeking money to pay utility bills. One day the aunt called Learned Lawyer, and asked for $103 to pay her electric bill.

Learned Lawyer responded, "I was just about to call you. My mother needs to borrow $140. Can you loan it to her?"

Silence greeted Learned Lawyer's appeal. Her aunt never again called requesting a loan. She eventually stopped gambling and then had the resources to pay her bills.

Try this the next time someone asks for a loan. Ignore their request and immediately turn the tables. You'll be surprised at how quickly this will end their calls. People who borrow do not want to loan money.

Tip 5: Do Not Enable Bad Habits

When we loan money to people, we enable their bad habits. Those with gambling addictions like the guy chased by the mob, the foreign widow, and Learned Lawyer's aunt are likely to ask for money.

Published Poet, introduced in the prior chapter as a person with a complicated spending history and credit profile, knows this only too well. When she lived in Las Vegas, her son frequently came up from Phoenix for the weekend, gambled away his paycheck, and sought her cash to get home. Published Poet took out a gas card, even though she doesn't drive, to help him. She gave her son money so many times that she estimated he owed her over $3000. She merely enabled his bad habits. If he had to hitchhike or walk home just once, he would have learned to save some of his money. Apparently, the town of Las Vegas keeps a slush fund for people like him. They put gamblers on a bus and give them $50 so they do not become a drain on their public resources.

New York City does this with immigrants who have become unemployed and lack the resources to return to their country. New York has elected to spend public money to fly these people home rather than risk having to support them long term.

Instead of flying people home, the country of Dubai gives people who have lost their jobs a month to leave the country or face imprisonment. Not surprisingly most people leave, often abandoning their cars at the airport.

Las Vegas, New York, and Dubai want people's money or labor, or both. They do not want to support them. Neither should you. People get themselves into fixes and it's not your responsibility to rescue them from the consequences of their behavior.

If you know someone with a gambling addiction, recommend they visit the website www.gamblersanonymous.org, which is founded on the same principles as Alcoholics Anonymous. Rather than enabling someone, suggest they seek help.

Tip 6: Do Not Rent Cars for People

It should go without saying, but do not rent cars for people. Even if they offer to pay the costs, you are loaning them your good name and credit worthiness. If someone is asking you to rent a car for them, it is because rental car companies have declared them unworthy to rent. Usually their credit is bad or driver's license disabled, or both. If rental car companies consider a person undeserving, you should not overrule that determination and put your own financial health at risk.

Further, by loaning rental cars you violate the clause in the contract that says only those individuals named on the paperwork can drive the car. If something goes wrong, the rental car company can sue you for negligent entrustment.

One Saturday, Learned Lawyer picked up a relative who used to borrow money without repaying it. To her surprise, this relative paid for their Chinese dishes at a mall food court. Over the meal, they discussed the relative's latest car accident. After lunch, the proverbial other shoe dropped.

The relative said, "I need a car for two days. Can you rent one for me? I'll pay you the cash up front."

"Hmm, why don't you just rent it yourself?" Learned Lawyer asked.

"I don't have a regular type of credit card. I have the type you have to put money on first," the relative replied.

"Oh," Learned Lawyer said, thinking this is the kind of credit card for people with financial difficulties. She removed some bills from her wallet and handed them to her relative. "Here's a $30 contribution to you taking cabs for the next two days. It's a gift. You do not have to pay it back."

The relative started laughing.

"My peace of mind is worth thirty dollars," Learned Lawyer said. "Although I know the car accidents never seem to be your fault, I don't want to worry about someone hitting you in a rental car."

The relative laughed some more, and they parted as friends. The relative didn't owe her anything, and Learned Lawyer held no resentment.

A year later, Learned Lawyer learned more details about her relative's car accident. It had taken place in a rental car, procured for him by his friend. The person told Learned Lawyer she had rented the car for him to take his kids trick or treating for Halloween. Unfortunately, the relative hit someone while driving on a revoked driver's license. The relative, the original renter, and the rental car agency were all sued. While the case ultimately settled, this is a situation to be avoided, as Learned Lawyer did.

If someone asks you to rent a car for them, simply say no, and run as fast as you can.

Tip 7: Give Away Money Only If You Want To

A friend of Learned Lawyer's once said she could think of only two reasons to do something: (1) you have to; or (2) you want to. Those individuals without substantial trust funds have to work. Those individuals with children have to support them. When relatives or friends ask to borrow money, you do not have to say yes. Do so only if you want to. Consider setting aside 10% of your income to share with others by responding to charitable appeals or to entreaties from friends and relatives. The choice is yours.

By giving generously of what you have and want to share, you create positive energy that will be returned many times over. It's tempting when resources are low to not share them. But that is when you should most redistribute some of your assets to others. If you only have half a candy bar left and someone looks at it longingly, offer that person a piece. This creates circulation in your life. If everything is energy, the more you generously give, the more will be returned to you.

Conversely, the more you loan and feel the immediate lack, the more you will potentially lose. If you decide that you do not want to give money, do not let someone "guilt trip" you into changing your mind. Simply tell them no, and walk away or end the conversation. There's no rule that says you have to respond. Do not provide an explanation. To do so is to invite a challenge, particularly from the gambling types.

Had Seattle Businessman, mentioned in Tip #1, taken this approach, would he have given out $7000 in cold cash? I doubt it. You shouldn't loan what you are unwilling to give. If you do decide to give money, do so with a generous spirit and open heart. Give money away if you have it and want to give it. This affords you emotional control because you have no expectation of a return and are happy to help.

Tip 8: Expect Ingratitude If You Give Money

You may think that if you generously give people money, instead of loaning it to them, they will be grateful. Often this is not the case. Usually you learn they received your check when it clears your bank account, not from a phone call or letter from them. Thus, there's no use worrying about whether people are going to thank you. Instead, as Dale Carnegie wrote in his book *How to Stop Worrying and Start Living*, you should expect ingratitude. Carnegie pointed out that of the seventy-eight people attorney Samuel Leibowitz saved from going to the electric chair, none ever thanked him.

If this attorney experienced ingratitude, you will as well. When the occasional thank-you note arrives in the mail or by email or text, rejoice. Unless someone has been raised to send notes of appreciation, like the first President George H.W. Bush who was known for his handwritten notes, it doesn't cross some people's minds to thank individuals who have been kind to them. They just accept the gift as their due.

Thus, give with no expectation of receiving words of appreciation. You'll feel less stress if you're not waiting on something that may never arrive.

Conversely, when you receive gifts—be they money, presents, or a meal—thank the giver. Gratitude should be happily cultivated in your life. You'll feel happier just writing a note and the receiver will want to do more to assist you.

Tip 9: Focus on Character and Document the Transaction If You Do Loan Money

While I advise against loaning money, there may be times when it's warranted. If you are considering doing this, focus on the borrower's character and not their reason nor their connection to you. Some people with strong characters hit rough patches and need funds to tide them over, particularly during recessionary times.

Wily Writer, a freelancer in her eighties, received a request to loan $6000 from a relative who fit such a description. She agreed to charge them seven percent interest when the going rate was 10%, and documented how the money would be repaid. All parties signed the contract. She was paid off in full, and they are still friends.

Having a contract will not help if you loan money to a person of dubious character. Learned Lawyer, for example, loaned money to a relative to buy a car and put the loan in writing. The relative did not pay it back. Her character was not as good as Wily Writer's relative, and the fact there was a document was of no help.

The advantage of having this paper is that you can write off the bad debts against your income taxes. To do so requires written documentation of the debt. If you have uncollected debts, you can research the issue through www.irs.gov or talk to a tax preparer about how you might write off your debt. This is not an ideal situation but it's better than a complete loss.

Further, please remember that age is not connected to character. Learned Lawyer loaned money to a relative when he was 18, and he did not pay it back. When the person turned 47, he put himself in a situation where he needed money. While he did not ask to borrow money and Learned Lawyer did not offer a loan, she did give him a gift. Later, the relative wrote, "I'll never forget what you did and I plan to pay back $125 a week until I repay you in full."

Learned Lawyer said nothing because she gave him the money and did not expect it to be returned. It's a good thing, too, because the relative did not make a single $125 payment. While this person had physically aged, his character had not changed. Do not make judgments based on people's age, gender, race, religion, or any other trait about them other than their character. That's all that counts.

Tip 10: Let Loaned Money Go

With rare exceptions, loaning money, be it to a friend or family member, is like tossing it into the wind and watching it fly away to parts unknown. You'd get more pleasure if you did this because then you could imagine how someone's day might be uplifted when they found a $20 bill as they walked to work.

When loaned funds are not returned, you resent the borrower and they dislike you. The relationship will sour to the point where the borrower avoids you at all costs. You will seek interaction, but find their phone has been disconnected or they have moved to another state with no forwarding address.

Rather than holding on to a situation that has flaws from its inception, let the money go and see how your life changes. I told Seattle Businessman if he let the money go, he would probably receive it back triple fold in another form, such as by landing new clients with even bigger accounts. His "friend" was in Gamblers Anonymous, and still didn't return his money.

Loaned money exemplifies what economists refer to as sunk costs. Once you have spent money on something, it's sunk, gone. Your decision should focus on what you should do today. You can ruminate about the money or let it go, and vow not to be taken the next time.

Better yet, think about the loaned money from the standpoint of the Law of Attraction, which is a spiritual concept that received considerable attention after "The Secret" DVD and best-selling book came out. In his book "The Law of Attraction," Michael Losier explains it simply as: what we think about, we vibrate in our desires and energy, whether positive or negative, comes back to us. By focusing on the failure of someone to repay borrowed money, the loaner is sending out the negative vibration of lack and that will generate more lack in that person's life.

Better to let the money go, as Reliable Realtor eventually did once she realized the foreign widow had a serious gambling problem and would never return the money. The sooner you release the loan and the expectation of being repaid, the better you will feel.

* * *

"Nor a lender be" is a piece of old wisdom to remember when it comes to requests to borrow money or to rent cars for others. It is not worth the ensuing headaches. Life can be stressful enough without having to worry about loans to others. The concluding advice in this chapter is to encourage you to answer truthfully all the questions in Table 2-1. Only if you are comfortable with the answers should you even consider making a loan.

Table 2-1: Questions to Consider Before Making Loans	
1.	Do you *have* to make this loan?
2.	Do you *want* to make this loan?
3.	Can you accept that this loan will never be repaid?
4.	Can you accept that this person might move or change phone numbers so you cannot reach him or her?
5.	Do you feel the borrower is of high moral character?
6.	Do you feel comfortable writing a contract so that you can deduct the amount on your taxes if it is not repaid?
7.	Will loaning the money negatively impact your financial well-being?

If you answer "No" to questions two, three, four, five and six, and/or "Yes" to question seven, then say "No" to the requester.

You will be grateful to yourself and will keep a friend who might have otherwise snuck away “like a thief in the night,” to quote from First Thessalonians Chapter 5, Verse 2.

CHAPTER 3

Spend Frugally

Juliet B. Schor's book *The Overspent American: Why We Want What We Don't Need* discusses "the cycle of work and spend." She postulates that American consumers are caught in a never-ending Ferris wheel, working hard to spend more to make up for the emptiness that comes from working too hard. Schor sent her research assistants to the town dump in a prosperous Boston suburb in search of the kinds of items the overspent American frequently discards. At the town dump, they found the following items in usable condition: a charcoal grill, a head board, a stroller, two lawn mowers, a table, a children's plastic playhouse, and several mattresses and box springs. The last items became hard to give away once big charities stopped accepting them.

Rather than contribute to such excess in dumpsters, consider photographer Craig Stephenson' approach to spending. He says, "My father told me when I was young if I spend less than I earn, I'd be rich. I now judge everything I buy based on how much freedom I'm going to lose by having to pay for it." For Stephenson, spending is directly linked to the energy it takes to earn the money to pay for the acquired item. If more people thought like Stephenson, they would purchase far fewer items.

Spending frugally requires strategically assessing purchases for big ticket items like cars, which will be discussed in *Chapter 4: Cars and Transportation Management,* and houses, which will be discussed in *Chapter 5: Home Sweet Home Finances.* This Chapter explores issues associated with personal spending on everything from apples to utilities and offers eight tips to improve your finances.

Tip 1: Budget Your Money

A budget, as set out in Table 3-1, indicates the amount of money coming in and going out. The income section should track all receipts such as those for salaries and wages, part-time jobs, business income, reimbursements, interests, and dividends. The expense section should include categories for savings, mortgage or rent, household upkeep and repairs, utilities (including gas, electricity, water, and telephone), Internet, cable, cell phone, credit cards, transportation expenses (car operating costs or public transportation), pets, subscriptions (magazines, newspapers, or websites), health care (prescriptions and insurance co-pays), child care, charitable donations or gifts, food (groceries and restaurants), and miscellaneous cash. Track miscellaneous expenses for several months to determine where your money goes.

Accounting for monthly budgets helps create ongoing financial plans. It also enables you to see at a glance if your outflow exceeds your inflow of cash.

Table 3-1: Monthly Budget			
Income		*Expenses*	
Salaries & Wages	$	Savings	$
Part-time Jobs	$	Mortgage or Rent	$
Business Income	$	Household upkeep	$
Reimbursements	$	Utilities	$
Interest	$	Internet	$
Dividends	$	Cable	$
		Cell phone	$
		Credit cards	$
		Transportation	$
		Pets	$
		Subscriptions	$
		Health care	$
		Child care	$
		Food	$
		Miscellaneous cash	$
Income Total	$	*Expense Total*	$

Tip 2: Notice That Small Items Add Up

Just a $3.50 coffee a day, or what author David Bach has termed the *latte* factor, costs $105 per month and $1260 a year. Ouch! If you're like Lively Law Student who feels he needs his java to perk up before morning classes, think how you could save $1000 per year if you purchase coffee supplies and a $40 electric coffee maker that turns on automatically and produces the coffee for you about the time you get out of bed. Awake to the aroma of your favorite coffee and bank $3 per day.

A lawyer told me about his taste for expensive alcohol, saying he frequently orders three $10 drinks when he goes out with friends several nights a week. When I pointed out that he was spending approximately $5000 a year on alcohol, he was astonished. Since he had also acknowledged not saving enough in his 401k, I suggested he switch to nursing one beer an evening and deposit the rest in his retirement account.

Coffee and alcohol can be purchased at a supermarket in many states. Even with Starbucks' items and beer, you'll find them more cheaply there. While at the grocery, spend the bulk of your cash on fresh items. Learn to cook. In grocery stores, shop the perimeter. The fresh items are there. The orange juice, milk and eggs are usually at the back, and the apples, carrots, and other fruits and vegetables to the side. Imagine the dollars these stores would lose if they put the most common items up front. People would grab what they came in for and leave. Instead, stores increase their profit margins by forcing people to walk the aisles.

Stores also place the most expensive products at eye level. When shopping for spaghetti sauce, for example, look to the lower shelves to find the least expensive sauce. This is where you will find the generic brands and discontinued items. If the sale-by date is still valid and you like the item, stock up.

Don't be lured into thinking that all items placed at the end of aisles are on sale. Often, manufacturers pay grocers additional fees to have their items placed on the end caps of aisles. While these items may appear to be on sale, most are not. They might offer one item (the chips, for example) at a discount while offering another item (the salsa) at a premium price that can be purchased cheaper elsewhere. Sneaky!

And then there's the tendency to buy on a whim. You'll find candy and gum at the register because these are impulse buys. People rarely make a special trip to a store to purchase mint gum, but if it's right in front of them they will grab a pack.

For your financial well-being, it's best to enter grocery stores with a list and stick to it. Some grocery stores have senior, student or military discount days. If you are in one of these categories and frequent a particular store, restrict your shopping to discount days to make you grocery money go further.

Coupons are considered *de classe* by some, but if you can pick up discounts on items normally purchased or would like to try, go for it. Two craft stores where I occasionally shop for art canvasses, brushes and other supplies, publish coupons worth 40% off one regularly priced item in the Sunday newspaper. I sometimes call neighbors and ask if they are going to use their coupon for that store. If not, I ask for it. If you are not friendly with your neighbors, it might be worth going online in search of the coupon or buying additional papers to get the discount. Smart phone apps have made this even easier because coupons can be downloaded, permitting cashiers to scan bar codes from smart phones. Because a newspaper clipping is not collected, you can reuse mobile coupons.

If you do not wish to deal with coupons, consider shopping at groceries that offer double-ad days. At stores like Sprouts, they overlap their ads. For example, their ads may run Wednesday to Wednesday, instead of the more traditional Wednesday to Tuesday. This means that everything from the prior ad and the new ad are on sale on Wednesday. This doubles the sale items available to you and makes shopping twice the fun. Ultimately, you will save thousands of dollars a year.

Tip 3: Buy in Bulk

For bulk purchases, you can save money by obtaining a Costco or Sam's Club card. These two companies are set up like warehouses to lower their costs and yours. Buying twelve packages of paper towels at a time, for example, is cheaper per unit than purchasing one as long as you possess the storage capacity. Notice, however, that these stores place the big ticket items like plasma televisions near the front to entice you upon entry and the low-margin goods at the opposite end of the store. Be prepared to go straight to the back to get what you need and not dilly-dally. Only purchase those items usable within a reasonable period of time, unless you can go with a friend and divide the purchases. Two young New Mexico attorneys shopped at Costco once a month and partitioned the spoils when they were single.

Tip 4: Shop Clothing Sales

With clothes, the goal is to buy great goods with cheap cash that make you look and feel fantastic. For discount hunting, be open to different types of stores, shopping the major sales at the high-end ones, taking a friend, and only spending cash. You can find junk at Saks Fifth Avenue or gold at Goodwill. You have to be willing to go there. You can buy a $700 designer bag at Nordstrom or a Tommy Hilfiger black leather purse in perfect condition for $5.00 at Goodwill. The reality is that no one will know what you paid for an item or where you bought it unless you tell them.

If you insist on shopping high-end stores, I recommend going to major sales. All stores, even those at the top of the fashion heap, eventually put items on sale. While visiting Nieman Marcus' Last Call outlet store on the outskirts of Phoenix, I once bought a brand new $900 silk skirt for $24.95. At Last Chance, a Nordstrom outlet store in Phoenix, I purchased a 100% silk lavender ball gown for $8.50 inclusive of tax. After a friend mentioned that she had paid the full price of $1200 for a Chanel bag that lasted 10 years, I told her I once bought two Gucci bags for 75% off, plus an additional 10% off, at Dillard's and they lasted 15 years. She responded, "Burr, you didn't buy those bags, you stole them." Not quite, but I loved that they lasted many seasons.

Buying quality merchandise saves time in the long run, and if you can purchase during sales, you obtain bragging rights. A colleague loved telling me she paid $10 for a dress I complimented. It was originally priced at $160.

When shopping for clothes, it can be helpful to go with a friend who will tell you the truth about how things look. This also increases the fun quotient. While at a National Federation of Press Women Conference in Richmond, Virginia, I split a cab fare with a journalist to go to the Richmond Goodwill. When I asked her to appraise a brown leather skirt that I managed to squeeze into, she said, "It would bother me that it keeps folding up at the top." I didn't buy it. Shopping with someone willing to give honest feedback can save you from purchasing something you later regret. As someone long ago said, "Even a bargain can cost you money."

Hard to believe but when it comes to clothes, *size doesn't matter*. You have to try things on. Designer merchandise tends to vary in dimensions. A colleague who normally wears a size twelve tried on a size-eight dress that fit. As she happily paid for the purchase, she said, "I can't believe I can wear a size-eight dress." This happens a lot because designer merchandise can be made with roomier dimensions.

Then, there's the "dance test." If you try on an item and start to move, buy it! If while trying on a new pair of shoes or dress your feet start grooving to the rhythm of the store music, it's for you. If a friend comments that you can't stop dancing while wearing something, consider purchasing it, particularly if the price is right.

Men can take advantage of the same bargains. Photographer Craig Stephenson purchased 20 Hawaiian shirts at a Honolulu Goodwill for $2–$3 each. They look great on him and he loved the price he paid. It left him more money to fund other aspects of his vacation.

Tip 5: Eliminate "Just in Case" Shopping

Author Judith Schiess Avila visited a friend who wanted to go shopping. They went to Mervyn's (now defunct) and the friend filled her cart. When they returned to the friend's house, she packed the items into a closet already overflowing with brand new packaged items she was keeping "just in case" she might need them someday.

A closet full of unused clothing just adds to the clutter afflicting lives and dragging down energy. Better to keep a smaller closet of items you love. Most people wear 20% of their wardrobe 80% of the time. The remainder rarely sees the light of day, and should be donated or sold to a consignment shop.

Tip 6: When Something Comes In, Something Should Go Out

To maintain your wardrobe at a comfortable level, consider adopting a personal rule that when something goes in, something must come out. Indeed, it's helpful to clean out your closet at least twice a year and donate items to the Goodwill or Salvation Army where they can become someone else's bargain find.

Tip 7: Shop with Cash

Perhaps the most important tip when it comes to clothes, food and all the smaller items: shop with cash only! Leave your debit and credit cards at home when you go on a shopping expedition. Decide what you can afford to spend, and take only that amount in cash. You'll enjoy your purchases longer if a bill doesn't show up a month later and you can't pay it. Nevertheless, if you have a credit card that offers benefits, such as airline miles, and you have the resources to pay the entire bill, then you should feel free to use your card.

Another reason to shop with cash is because of cyber thieves who hack major stores like Target, looking for credit and debit card information to steal. In November 2013, the thieves aimed their computers at Target the day before Black Friday and continued until they were discovered on December 15, eighteen days later. In the interim, they captured data for over 40 million individuals. Had you been a Target shopper who paid with cash, you would not have to worry about the purloining of your data. There would have been none to seize.

Tip 8: Remember to Be Frugal, Not Cheap

Being frugal is not cheap. Frugality means you are careful with how you spend your money while maintaining the comforts of life. Cheap indicates you save money no matter who you inconvenience, even yourself.

Southwest Airlines is a great example of creatively frugal. They were handing out peanuts when other airlines were providing full meals. Southwest advertised that compromising on food permitted them to offer lower airfares. When the recession hit the airline industry, Southwest Airlines was still handing out peanuts and had added pretzels and other snack items while other airlines ceased to serve any food, even peanuts.

Tip 9: If You Become a Compulsive Shopper, Seek Assistance

If you shop to calm emotional hurts, consider Published Poet's story. Her home overflowed with items from Wal-Mart, Kmart, Target, and J.C. Penny's (or JCP). Catalogs crammed her mailbox at an average of three per day. She ordered from them all, causing packages to arrive on a daily basis. The QVC Network was her favorite television channel. She was quick to pick up the phone to order before an item sold out. As a consequence, she accumulated over 150 pairs of shoes, thousands of clothing items, hundreds of boxes of crayons, and several hundred skeins of yarn, notebooks and books. It all piled up in her one bedroom apartment to the point where finding a path from her front door to her living room couch became a hop-scotch expedition. When Published Poet's daughter moved her to another city, she gave away the accumulation. As Published Poet's daughter placed yet another load to be given away in the senior center community room, one of Published Poet's neighbors commented, "She was living in a store."

If a store has taken up residence in your living space, you may have a problem. Psychiatrists and psychologists diagnose it as "Compulsive Buying Disorder," a disease that was mentioned briefly in the Diagnostic Statistical Manual III as associated with impulse control. People with CBD feel compelled to shop and spend in quantity, according to Dr. Donald Black in his article "A review of Compulsive Buying Disorder" in the 2007 World Psychiatry Journal.

Dr. Black says that medications cannot be relied upon to combat Compulsive Buying Disorder. Rather, he recommends patients (a) admit they have CBD; (b) get rid of credit cards and checkbooks; (c) shop with friends or relatives who do not have CBD; and (d) find meaningful ways to spend their leisure time other than shopping. The bottom line is that while shopping within your means can be fun, compulsive buying is a disease that needs curing.

If packages are piling up in a relative or friend's home, suggest a psychologist. Published Poet's daughter found a counselor for her mother by calling numbers listed in the yellow pages for psychologists and asking for recommendations. The daughter located a psychologist willing to work with someone with compulsive buying disorder. The therapy process resembled that for alcoholics and other addicts, requiring Published Poet to acknowledge that her debt had become a problem and then taking steps to resolve it. The sessions began weekly. As Published Poet reduced her shopping expeditions and improved her finances, the sessions lessened to every other week, then once a month, and finally every other month.

Checking in periodically with her therapist reminded Published Poet to not go to her previously favorite stores or malls. From some chains and catalogs, Published Poet accepted a lifetime ban, recognizing that she could not enter these environments without resuming her compulsive buying behavior. Once she gave up credit cards, QVC television purchases ceased.

Fortunately for most readers of this book, the situation has not become that dire. Take a page from Craig Stephenson's book and think of purchases from the perspective of how much energy (i.e. working hours) will be needed to pay for them. Buy less and enjoy what you do purchase.

CHAPTER 4

Car and Transportation Management

Managing your transportation needs can crimp styles and empty wallets if individuals are not careful. You do not want to become the kind of hounded debtor who backs her car into stalls license plate first to stay one step ahead of Repo Man. Eventually he will catch on, and the debtor will walk out the door one day to find her car has disappeared, along with several personal items. Use the following tips to educate yourself about alternative transportation possibilities and car purchases so that a car serves you and not you it.

Tip 1: Explore Cheaper Means of Transportation

Save money by taking public transportation, carpooling, biking, or walking to your destination. Do an honest assessment of how much it cost you to get to work. Then ask yourself: Can I get there cheaper? If there is someone at work who lives near you? Can you share the driving several days a week? What would public transportation cost? Are there buses, subways, light rails, or trains near you? If you do so, you might arrive less stressed than if you drove yourself.

If you live within two to three miles of your work or grocery stores, you can easily bike. If you live within a mile and a half, you can walk. With the latter two transportation methods, you exercise your muscles and will arrive mentally fresh.

Any savings can go into your emergency fund to rent a car when necessary or a fun fund for something you want.

Tip 2: Shop for Cars with Your Mind Open and Your Wallet Hidden

When public or free transportation is not available for the bulk of daily needs, most individuals require cars to travel to jobs, chores, and so forth. With new cars costing $25,000 and more, far too many approach this purchase haphazardly. Remar Sutton's book *Don't Get Taken Every Time* provides excellent advice on how to buy and lease new and used cars. Sutton spent decades in the automobile industry before exposing the numerous methods that dealers use to fleece unsuspecting customers. One of his most important recommendations is to negotiate with knowledge by acquiring the invoice price the dealer paid for a new car through websites like www.consumerreports.com, www.edmunds.com, or www.kbb.com (for Kelly Blue Book). You can also purchase car guidebooks or borrow them from your local library.

This information enables you to negotiate upwards from what the dealer paid rather than downwards from a sticker price inflated with unnecessary add-ons, like $100 for detailing (or cleaning and waxing) the car. A new car should arrive ready to go with new paint and a clean engine from the manufacturer. Even when car dealers advertise they are going out of business, don't be fooled into thinking they will automatically lower their prices.

While some seem to be giving good deals, be wary of those who artificially inflate prices in order to appear to be marking them down. They are well aware of the human psychology that tends to think in relative terms, rather than absolutes. That is why it is best to acquire the dealer invoice price before arriving at the showroom floor.

You can also call car stores within a comfortable radius of your home. If you live in a small city, you may obtain a better deal in a medium or large city. Go to the manufacturer's website and do a search for the car stores near you. Tell them the car, the color and other details that you are looking for and obtain a quote. Learned Lawyer did this, and found that a car store fifty-five miles north of where she lives had the car she sought. They sold it to her at $400 above dealer invoice price. This works best if you are paying cash or have previously secured your financing for a car.

Tip 3: Shop Car Financing Before Searching

Another tip is to shop for financing before searching for a new or used car. This enables you to compare finance rates with what the dealer may offer. At the same time, you should make sure you have adequate funds to buy the car in its entirety or that a car payment fits your budget. This is particularly important during times of tight credit. Know your financing options.

Some dealers have been known to falsify records in order to get people with poor or no credit history approved for loans. This happened to my eighteen-year-old nephew with unfortunate consequences. He ended up returning the car he couldn't pay for, yet he remained liable for the loan. The incident showed up on his credit report as a voluntary surrender. I had sent Nephew a copy of Remar Sutton's book *Don't Get Taken Every Time*, but he never opened it. Just like you can bring a horse to water but you can't make it drink, some people can have good advice at their fingertips and fail to open the pages. If Nephew had obtained his own financing, then he could have avoided this problem.

Tip 4: Have Mechanics Check Out Used Cars Before Purchasing

When buying a used car, be sure to have a mechanic check it out. Kicking the tires is an inadequate mechanical check. There are two checklists in Remar Sutton's book *Don't Get Taken Every Time*, one for the individual to perform and one for the mechanic. My rule of thumb is the car has to pass the basic checklist before I will pay for a mechanic's pre-purchase inspection. If the mechanic returns with a list of more than three items wrong or any problems in major systems, I let the car go.

I once ignored this rule, and subsequently paid out my regrets. I became so tired of searching for a car that I bought one that a mechanic said had problems with its air conditioning and clutch. He said they could be easily fixed. Initially the repairs were inexpensive, but eventually it cost over a thousand dollars to replace the air conditioning compressor and another thousand to replace the clutch (twice). Yikes! The initial mechanic's check raised red flags. When these are waved at you, better to head in another direction.

Tip 5: Budget for the Car's Upkeep

Cars require weekly, monthly, bi-yearly, and sometimes annual costs. Estimate these before purchasing a vehicle. On a weekly or bi-weekly basis, you will be spending money for gas to run the car. Individuals with limited budgets should consider purchasing only those vehicles that obtain at least 30 miles per gallon on the highway.

When gas prices exceeded $4 a gallon during 2008, 2012, and 2013, many individuals who had bought gas-guzzling SUVs could no longer afford to drive them. People like Joyful Judge loved their Hummers, but traded them when they cost $100 or more to fill them up. General Motors closed its Hummer division in 2012, eight months after entering into bankruptcy reorganization.

Worse still, some SUV owners had to drive to three different stations to fill their bottomless tanks. They ran into a problem because many credit cards have a $50 or $75 limit at gas stations. Credit card companies place this restraint to limit their liability in case a card gets stolen. For the same reason, many gas stations now ask purchasers to key in their zip code. Even when gas costs less than $2 per gallon, purchasing a low consumption vehicle helps balance your budget. When it costs less than $20 to fill up your tank, you'll laugh all the way home.

Budget for maintenance and repairs. A new car requires mostly oil changes and tire rotations for the first couple of years. A used car will eventually require tune-ups and more expensive repairs. Set aside a certain amount annually for maintenance and repairs, say $100 to $200 per month, depending on the type of vehicle, so you will have the money to pay $1000 to replace a clutch. Budgeting monthly for an occasional expense lowers stress levels.

Tip 6: Shop Insurance Rates

Insurance rates vary considerably depending on the car model and the driver's record. After you've narrowed your search to certain models, call your insurance agent to determine the bill for the cars that interest you. For some models, the rates may be so high as to discourage pursuing those cars. Red cars usually require higher insurance premiums, probably for the same reasons they attract more speeding tickets. People feel emboldened when driving them.

Years ago, Learned Lawyer bought a red Mazda Miata as a second car to her Honda Civic. When she sold the Civic, the insurance went up 25% more than what she previously paid to insure both cars with the Miata as her back-up car. She nicknamed the Miata her man-attracting car, but the men it most attracted were cops writing speeding tickets. She finally sold it.

Of course anyone can obtain speeding tickets in any vehicle if driving fast enough. It's best to slow down and obey the posted limits. You will probably get there about the same time with less stress if you do. Indeed, if you have a need to speed, go kart racing or join a club where it's legal and fun to speed on dedicated tracks.

Also, try to obtain insurance from reputable companies, such as State Farm, Allstate or Farmer's. Attorney Peter Romero, who specializes in assisting individuals who have been injured in car accidents, opines, "State Farm is the best. They are easy to deal with and always negotiate in good faith." He says that the insurance companies no one has ever heard of are to be avoided because they specialize in insuring high risk individuals and then trying to evade liability once a claim is filed.

If you are hit by someone who is insured by such a company, try working with your own insurance company and let them seek reimbursement from the other company. Your car will get fixed faster and you can seek medical treatment sooner. Plus, you will have fewer hassles if you don't have to deal with a company trying to blame you for an accident that a police officer has already determined was their insured's fault. Call the police if anyone is injured or there is significant damage to your vehicle or both. It's helpful to have a neutral party assess the situation and determine fault.

Other individuals have had success with AARP and GEICO. Writer Phil Jackson said his AARP rate was a third of what he paid to insure through State Farm. Author Melanie Groves raves about GEICO for their customer service. She said after her car was twice stolen and once broken into, GEICO immediately stepped in to assist her. You can get GEICO insurance quotes by contacting the website www.geico.com. You must become a member (open to individuals age 50 and older) to be eligible for AARP insurance rates.

When your insurance bill arrives, you can elect to pay it in full or divide the payments over several months. Happily write that check.

CHAPTER 5

Home Sweet Home Finances

During nearly forty years as a top musical artist, the late Michael Jackson accumulated over $700 million in income. He mortgaged his home, Neverland, which cost him $7,000,000 a year in upkeep. When he ran into financial difficulties, he tried to sell Neverland to eliminate the $20 million mortgage and the upkeep costs. Whether you have hit the equivalent of the performance lottery like Jackson, or are just starting out like your neighbor musician, be careful to mind your home finances. This becomes even more important during times of economic downturn such as the worldwide economy faced beginning in 2007. Everyone from rock stars to ordinary people can encounter financial issues with homes.

This Chapter divides into three parts: acquiring the home, mortgage and upkeep finances, and selling the home. My advice comes from analyzing problems that others and myself have experienced with searching for, buying, and selling homes. The information in this Chapter will serve you well, whether you are in a buyer's market when there are tons of homes available and few shoppers or a seller's market when there are few homes available and tons of shoppers.

Part A. Acquiring Your Dream Home

Tip 1: Find the Money

While it may be tempting to search for a home without thinking about the costs or discussing money with a spouse, banker or other financial advisors, don't make this mistake. It's fun to window shop for homes, be it on the Internet or stopping by open houses, but don't get carried away. In your housing search, it's important to know the top limit of what you can afford, what mortgage payment would feel comfortable, and which one would be an absolute strain on your budget. This could make a difference between buying a dream home and never vacationing again (commonly known as "house poor") or buying that less expensive condo and traveling to an island in the summer and a ski resort in winter. Your values will determine what works best for you. Some people prefer to live in luxury on a daily basis and forego vacations. Others opt for a modest dwelling so they can travel often and sometimes in style. Through frugal management of resources, some can live and travel well.

In either case, look for houses within your complete price range, but do not tell your realtor your top price. As most agents get paid a percentage of the sale, they benefit when you spend more. Further, make a budget of current spending habits that includes rent or mortgage, utilities, upkeep, and other actual costs. This gives you a sense of what's comfortable and how much additional money you will need.

Talk to your banker or mortgage broker to obtain pre-approval for a mortgage if you will need one. Keep in mind that you will need a down payment and closing costs, including points to obtain your mortgage. To avoid paying mortgage insurance, your down payment should equal or exceed 20% of the purchase price. Your mortgage will then just include principal, interests, taxes, and insurance. Mortgage pre-approval helps your bargaining position as it indicates to potential sellers that you can afford your offer price.

During the buying frenzy that peaked between 2004 and 2006, bankers were known to make loans to people with no jobs, no income, and no assets. These became known as NINJA loans. Those days gave way to the credit crunch of 2008 and 2009 when banks became stingy about even loaning to people with decent credit. Having a solid financial base and excellent credit will help you even in the worst of times.

Tip 2: Establish Your Criteria

After figuring how much you can afford, choose a location or several neighborhoods that interest you. The list in Table 5-1 helps you zero in on what is important to you.

Table 5-1: Home Shopping Criteria	
Location	Is the home near your work or children's schools? Are there nearby groceries and fun activities? Does the home come with nature or city views? Does the home let in a lot of light, or is it dark?
Type	Do you prefer a condo, co-op, townhouse, row house, or ranch?
Square Footage	Is the home large enough for your needs? Is the home too large to keep up?
Stories	Do you desire one, two, or more levels?
Bedrooms	What is your preference? One, two, three, or more?
Bathrooms	How many are required? One, two, three, or more?

Amenities	Do you want a garage or assigned parking spaces? If so, for how many cars? Do you want a luxurious master bathroom? Do you desire a gourmet kitchen?

Draft a simple list that includes the type of home you prefer, the square footage, garage or parking areas, single or multiple stories, as well as the number of bedrooms and bathrooms. Note preferred amenities. By establishing desires in advance, you'll know when you find them.

As you have probably heard, the three most important factors in selecting real estate are location, location, and location. Don't forget to consider your commute to work and to schools if you have children. The closer you live to your job and schools, the more time, energy, and money you save getting there. When gas prices exceeded $4 per gallon during 2008, 2012, 2013, and 2014, some individuals with gas-guzzling vehicles who lived sixty miles from work found it cost them more to get there than they made after taxes on minimum wage earnings. A vehicle getting 10 miles to the gallon was costing $48 round trip a day, or $240 a week and $12,480 a year. Be sure to check out homes in neighborhoods close to where you work. If you can walk or bike to where you earn your livelihood, you will enjoy the journey and get or stay in shape at the same time.

Ultimately, a love-at-first-sight feeling may come over you that says this is the one. While these feelings are helpful, go back and check the home against your must-have and hoping-to-get criteria. A good feeling, coupled with a home that meets your list, may indicate you have found the dream home for you. On the other hand if the house feels wrong, consider passing although it meets all of your criteria. Your gut might be telling you something your eyes have missed.

Tip 3: Shop the Right Seasons

Spring and summer are usually the best seasons for home shopping because availability is highest then. Sellers place more homes on the market during these times as families seek to move while kids are out of school. During good times, prices tend to be higher and interest rates rise as more buyers seek mortgages. Still, there are advantages to shopping off season and during recessionary times.

In fall and winter, prices decline for lack of buyers, and sellers become motivated after houses did not receive offers during high-selling seasons. Further, shopping in winter can help you obtain information about whether the home is weather-proof. If you walk into a brand new home the day after a rainstorm and there is a leak in the living room ceiling, that is a bad sign. Even if you love the look of the home and the location, walk away. This is just the first signal of shoddy construction. If you insist on buying it anyway, prepare to periodically call repair men and live in constant frustration.

In a recessionary era, there will be lots of homes available year round with low prices. In Scottsdale, Arizona, for example, homes that previously sold for $336,000 were being auctioned at a starting bid of $56,000 in 2010. Homes in nearby Phoenix were being auctioned at even lower starting prices ranging from $15,000 to $25,000 for homes that previously sold for $125,000 to $250,000. On eBay and directly, buyers were picking up homes for hundreds of dollars in Detroit and thousands of dollars in Cleveland.

The old adage—buy low, sell high—still applies. If you can pick up a home for a song because of a market glut and it works for your budget, go for it. When the Phoenix metropolitan area recovered, for example, some earlier buyers earned double returns or more on their initial investments.

Be wary, however, of buying a home sight unseen. Auction buying requires you to investigate the home in advance as much as possible to avoid acquiring a lemon. Some of the successful eBay bidders later found out their bargain purchase for $3500 had been condemned and would cost another $8000 to raze to the ground and start over.

Tip 4: Check Out Incentives

Look into whether you qualify for government incentives, which permit you to deduct specified amounts from the taxes you would normally pay. In 2009 and 2010, for example, the federal government offered an $8000 incentive to first-time home buyers and a $6500 incentive to those who had lived in their homes for at least five years. To qualify for the full amount, the home purchase price could not exceed $800,000 and the income of the buyer had to be $125,000 or less. If income exceeded $125,000, then the incentive phased out. The person could wait until paying their next year's taxes to obtain the tax credit or immediately lower the withholding to receive more money back in their current paychecks.

State and local governments periodically offer incentives to encourage low income buyers. By lowering the amount you ultimately have to pay for a home, incentives can make a home affordable. Nevertheless, be sure to check all requirements associated with incentives.

Tip 5: Get Assistance

Realtors are as easy to find as dating services. Their ads may appear in your email in-box, by snail mail, or on a flyer attached to your door. Search for them on the Internet. Ask friends to recommend their realtor. Proceed with care, however, as what works for one person may not work for all. I recommended Rita, my realtor, to some friends, and she fired them as clients after becoming suspicious as to whether they had actually terminated their relationship with their former realtor. She called the former realtor and discovered he thought they were still his clients. This is the equivalent of realtor double dating, and one of them is bound to be stiffed of a commission fee.

To obtain an appropriate realtor, interview several to find someone who is trustworthy and will keep your best interest in the forefront. Ask them about their client numbers. If they currently have more than 20 clients, they may not have the time to assist you. Ask them about their negotiation skills. As a buyer, you will be looking for the best value. Make sure the realtor doesn't mind writing up low offers. One realtor told me that the most she could negotiate was $7000 off a seller's price. I was startled by her statement of a flat number and did not hire her. On the home I bought, I negotiated nearly $15,000 off the seller's price because Rita was willing to write the contract. That said, in a hot market, your realtor may advise you to write an offer that exceeds the asking price if she determines that the seller has already received multiple offers.

Further, get a sense of whether you like the realtor and wouldn't mind spending time with him or her. If a realtor is slovenly in appearance, you may want to find another as he or she may be slipshod in looking after your interests.

I retained Rita because of her honesty. A friend recommended her after I complained that my current realtor had failed to submit an offer. When I called Rita to ask her to submit the offer, she asked about the location. After I told her, she replied, "Absolutely not. I do not represent sellers or buyers in that complex. It's built on a landfill."

After I picked myself up off the floor, I hired Rita. She was the last realtor I retained to help me in my seven-year off-and-on search to purchase a new home. Rita's philosophy was that she would never sell clients homes that she could not resell for them. If we turned a corner and she found a home backed up to a major street, she would keep driving. I once inquired why she had not shown me a particular home after I saw a sale sign on the front lawn.

She barked, "Don't you see those power lines? Can't you hear that freeway noise? You'll never be able to resell that home. Now come on."

After that moment, I nicknamed 4′11″ Rita "The General." She kept me focused on finding the home that met my criteria and made clear she would not sell me a potential disaster.

Finally, consider finding a realtor who has been in the business a long time. These realtors know the locations of former landfills and toxic waste. When I sold my Phoenix condo, the realtor informed me that according to the Environmental Protection Agency the groundwater had been polluted by an industrial plant. She also informed me that the Environmental Protection Agency said the drinking water in central Phoenix did not come from groundwater. When I expressed concern, she said, "Don't worry. Scottsdale is also sitting on toxic waste and it hasn't affected sales there." This was important information from someone who had been around a while. Since toxic sites are constantly being cleaned up, one should check on the current status of the areas that interest you.

Tip 6: Inspect Before Committing

When you settle on a home you like, condition your offer on satisfactory roof, radon, structural, termite, and other inspections. If these investigations uncover problems, you can ask the seller to correct them or lower the price if you wish to proceed with the sale. In a hot market, the seller may refuse to correct the problems. You have to decide if you love the house enough to eat the additional costs.

In a normal market or a buyer's market, you can ask the seller to provide a home warranty package to guarantee the major systems of your new home for one year. The goal for you is not to fall completely in love with the home until after the inspections, and the sale is complete. That way if there are serious problems, you can let go without breaking your heart. A better deal will greet you around the corner.

Tip 7: Accept What You Cannot Change

It is tempting to walk into a home and think about making major changes such as adding or tearing down walls, carpeting brick floors, cutting down exposed beams, or trimming the neighbor's tree to improve the view. Think twice. If you have to change fundamentally the structure of a house, then it may not be right for you. Be willing to let it go. Another will come along that is more appropriate for your needs. Accept what you cannot change and move on.

Cosmetic changes are another story. Consider overlooking 1970's green carpet or 1950's cabinetry to see the essence of a structure. A $25 gallon of paint can make a huge difference in the look and feel of a room. Sellers seeking the highest prices will make these cosmetic changes before you see the home. As a buyer, you can save a lot of money if you're willing to purchase a fixer-upper that just needs painting, re-carpeting, and other cosmetic changes.

Tip 8: Be Grateful for the Ones That Got Away

Sometimes we mourn when our dream house sells to another buyer or the seller rejects our offer. This could be a blessing in disguise. I mentioned that I retained Rita after she refused to submit an offer on a townhouse in a complex that was built on a landfill. That was at least the sixth home within that complex that I had contemplated buying. Every single offer fell apart for one reason or another. After I met Rita, I became grateful I had not bought a home on a landfill that had been a city construction dump. I had thought the complex stable because it appeared to perch on the top of a mountain. What lay underneath was garbage.

Others have bought homes on reclaimed land only to face ongoing structural issues with the foundation cracking, the windows separating from the frame, and the walls slanting. These issues are expensive to fix. Before purchasing, hire a structural engineer to analyze the house. This will cost additional funds but could be worth it in the long run if you avoid purchasing a home with structural issues.

Tip 9: Negotiate the Contract

After you establish what you would like to offer for the home, calculate three prices: (1) the initial offer that you plan to make to the seller; (2) the price you hope the seller will accept; and (3) the top price you are willing to pay. The last is particularly important if you buy at an auction, a frequent method for selling foreclosed homes. To avoid succumbing to auction fever, you must set a price in advance by which you are not willing to exceed. Do not get caught in the frenzy of the moment and pay more than you think the property is worth.

Most two-party negotiations end in the middle range between the seller's asking price and the buyer's initial offer. Thus, your initial offer should leave room to move up toward your hoping-to-get price. Of course, if the seller perceives your initial offer to be too low (especially in a hot market), he or she may reject your offer and not submit a counteroffer. Don't despair if this happens to the home of your dreams as you can write another offer that's closer to the seller's price, providing you do not compromise your budget.

Further, read the contract in its entirety, including the fine print. Have your realtor or attorney explain any items or terms you do not understand. You need to know the parameters of your agreement, particularly if buying an adjustable rate mortgage that can increase significantly over time. Many people in the house buying frenzy of 2004–2006 signed contracts containing clauses that doubled or tripled their mortgage payments in a matter of months. Most of these individuals saw their homes foreclosed when they could not afford increased monthly charges.

Don't be afraid to ask your realtor for a price calculation of all the fees associated with your offer, including real estate taxes. It's crucial to know your total costs, including all closing costs and mortgage fees necessary to complete the transaction so you are not taken by surprise.

Part B. Home Finances

Tip 10: Pay Off the Mortgage

Because income for many can be sporadic during both recessionary and good times, most people, if they can afford it, would benefit by buying homes outright rather than incurring debt. While entertainers may receive millions for deals for their services, some of us receive windfalls through gifts, bonuses, inheritances, hitting the lottery, or sales of appreciated assets such as previous homes. When large amounts appear unexpectedly, consider using the new-found cash to buy a home that will be yours completely.

If, however, you can only buy a home by obtaining a mortgage, then commit to paying it off as soon as possible. Even those with stable income may find themselves downsized in a sudden shift of economic fortunes. Prepare for this eventuality by saving and paying off your mortgage during good times.

This advice flies in the face of conventional wisdom advising people to incur as much mortgage debt as they possibly can to obtain the highest tax deduction. Indeed, when I have given this advice at seminars, folks in the audience or other panelists have argued with me. I stood my ground.

Real estate markets are cyclical. Some folks have only bought and sold in up markets, and believe prices only increase. When markets fall, they can wreak havoc on home finances.

Decades ago, Learned Lawyer bought a one-bedroom condominium in Phoenix, Arizona, for $42,000. By the time she sold it in nine years later, she had paid $41,000 in mortgage payments, yet only $1,500 went to reduce principal leaving a balance of $39,500. Unfortunately, the real estate market for condos had gone south and the condo was only worth $20,000 in the open market (*see* Table 5-2).

Table 5-2: Phoenix Condo Finances

Year	Value	Mortgage Balance
1	$42,000	$42,000
9	$20,000	$39,500

If Learned Lawyer had accepted an offer at fair market value, she would have needed to cough up an additional $19,500 to sell the condo. What saved her was that she had obtained a no-qualifying, fully assumable loan and could just have a buyer assume the payments. These loans no longer exist because the Federal Housing Authority (FHA) ceased making them.

Many people buying a home ignore the fine print that says taking out a 30-year mortgage could lead to paying twice as much interest as principal. Had Learned Lawyer continued paying on that condo for the full 30 years, she would have paid the bank over $80,000 in total interest in addition to the original $42,000 in principal. In essence, she would have paid three times the original value.

When obtaining a mortgage, aim for the shortest term that is comfortable for your budget, be it 10, 15, 20, 25, or 30 years. If you obtain a conventional 30-year mortgage, commit to paying it off in five or 10 years at most. With the home that my realtor Rita helped me purchase, I committed to pay it off in five years so that I could be debt-free once again. You should make a similar promise to yourself and fulfill it. I applied any additional income that came my way from speaking, writing, or selling my artwork to the mortgage. I also was careful about my finances during this time to lessen expenses so there would be more income to apply to the mortgage.

Some individuals think that while they are doing well, there will probably come a time when their finances could dramatically shift. Michael Jackson went from being the top performer in the 1980s and 1990s to a pariah by 2000 after being charged with child molestation. At the same time, his finances deteriorated due to massive spending and failure to properly invest his assets. Before his untimely death at age 50, he tried to sell Neverland which had fallen into disrepair when he could not afford the upkeep. His plan to give concerts in London was conceived to revive his finances.

Do not be like Michael Jackson. Prepare ahead of time for the moment when your finances could drastically shift by buying a home with cash or paying off the mortgage as soon as possible. When the economic downturn accelerated in 2008 and 2009, those who owned their homes were able to live unworried about paying a monthly mortgage or facing eviction. They just needed to timely pay taxes and insurance. Without pressure to sell or relocate, you can remain in your home until prices recover.

Tip 11: Be Careful of Monthly Expenses and Maintenance Costs

When it comes to *horses,* the conventional wisdom is that they are easy to acquire, expensive to maintain, and hard to get rid of. Fortunately, houses do not always follow this horse-sense, as a buyer may have a variety of expenses. I mentioned that the yearly upkeep for Michael Jackson's Neverland Ranch was $7,000,000. This paid for the insurance, utilities, staff, and maintenance.

The size of a place can make a huge difference in its maintenance cost. When it comes to square footage, 3000 seems to be the cutoff for a house that a family can clean on their own if they desire. Above 3000 square feet and the family will most likely seek weekly, bi-weekly, or daily maid service, and weekly or monthly gardening assistance depending on the type of lot. The larger the space, the more assistance you will need. The busier you become, the more likely the need to hire housekeepers, cooks, nannies, and other assistants. As the staff mushrooms, so do the monthly and yearly maintenance costs. Pools can become an attractive nuisance for neighborhood youth seeking a cool uninvited dip on a hot summer's day. Further, they increase maintenance and insurance costs.

During an economic downturn, many high income individuals lose their jobs and become forced to lay off their domestic staff or cut their hours. With any home, people should ask themselves: If I had to maintain this myself, could I? If the answer is no, buy something smaller.

Part C. Renting or Selling Homes

The time may come when you need to move suddenly or decide to acquire an additional home while keeping the current one. In both situations, renting is a good option, particularly if you anticipate returning some day or if you seek passive income, the payment of checks for which you do not actively labor. My great-grandmother, her sisters and daughters were active practitioners of the passive income approach. They rented rooms and houses to others. Indeed, for two of my great-grandmother's sisters, this was their sole source of income. Whether renting or selling, you will need to prepare the realty and yourself for the transition.

Tip 12: Prepare Your Home

Renting or selling real estate can be as stressful as buying. You will need to prepare your home by cleaning it up, clearing clutter, fixing broken items, and enhancing the curb appeal. The saying that "cleanliness is next to godliness" bears much truth in the selling of real estate. Nothing turns a potential renter or buyer off more than to walk through the front door of a home and be confronted with the smell of cat urine, parrot feces, and the grunginess of accumulated dirt. Cat urine can be particularly problematic if it has been inserted into the interior walls and hard wood floors. This may necessitate wall and floor removal and rebuilding to eliminate the stench. Just as most people would not want to go out on a first date without showering first, they should consider the impact of the un-showered home on the potential buyer.

Papers lying about amidst a thousand un-shelved books do not appeal. Potential renters or buyers want to envision their belongings in the new space and find this difficult if a home overflows with clutter. Some sellers pay staging services to clean up their home and make it hospitable for potential buyers. Sellers can reap thousands of dollars in additional profit if buyers view their home as turn-key ready; that is, the new owner will simply need to put the key in the door and move right in.

If you can't afford a staging service, ask your realtor for recommendations and take his or her advice. If the grout on the tile needs scrubbing or the carpet needs to be pulled up, be prepared to do so or pay local contractors. Also, watch TV shows like "Sell this House" to pick up tips. Put the best face on your home, the same way a screenwriter would clean up a script and a musician would put out a CD with his best music.

Look also at other properties in your neighborhood to determine what upgrades they are offering. If granite countertops have become the norm in your neighborhood, upgrade yours while you have time to enjoy them.

This becomes all the more important during an economic downturn when you will be competing with many available unsold homes. Since you get one chance to make a first impression, it's best to have a fabulous looking and smelling home greet any potential buyer. Some renters or buyers are particular about the front yard and the front door. If they are disheveled or dirty, they assume the house will be so as well and may not even enter the home.

Tip 13: Prepare Yourself

Your house may rent or sell quickly, giving you only 30-45 days to find a new home. What are you going to do? Get prepared by surveying the available homes or rentals in your new location. If you plan to buy, review all the tips in the section on buying real estate.

Conversely, during recessionary times your home may sit for a long time, several months if not years. If you have to move for job reasons, negotiate with your employer to assist in the selling of your home to alleviate the negative economic impact. Be prepared to lower your price. There's always a renter or buyer somewhere, it's just a matter your willingness to negotiate.

In recessionary times, it is not unheard of for buyers to seek 25%, 35%, or higher discounts. In some areas particularly hit by the downturn, sellers lowered prices by 50%.

Buyers may request other concessions, such as the payment of their closing costs, or funds to change windows, carpets, paint and so forth.

Sellers should not take any of these demands personally. Buyers are simply trying to get the best deal possible to hedge against a further downturn in the market. For some sellers, discounts and concessions are worth it to unload the home. If their finances are in order, particularly for those who have paid off their mortgage, sellers can either choose to negotiate or wait to sell another day when prices rise again, as they likely will.

Tip 14. Carefully Consider Options When Your Home Is Underwater

During the Great Recession, many individuals found their homes underwater; that is, worth less than the remaining mortgage. In many instances, a lot less like the Phoenix condo in Table 5-2. The *Miami Herald* reported on 24 October 2009 that Andres Duque had paid $125,000 for his condo, thinking he got a bargain for it in 2005. By 2009, similar units sold for $35,000 or even less. Duque chose to walk. He stopped paying the mortgage and the bank foreclosed.

This would be a difficult choice for many individuals. There is the ethos permeating many moral lives that requires honoring promises, including those made by signing contracts to take out loans and repay them. Indeed, one professor conducted a survey that revealed 87% of Americans think it's immoral to default on a mortgage just because they live in a home with negative equity. [See Brent T. White, The Morality of Strategic Default, UCLA Law Review Discourses, Forthcoming Arizona Legal Studies Discussion Paper No. 10–15 (May 22, 2010).]

Other Americans would not consider walking away because they adore their home with its many memories making it unique to them, even though it may have the same floor plan as the house next door that sold for hundreds of thousands of dollars less. This is a choice only the individuals involved can make, but pressure is mounting to walk as more commentators make the economic argument for doing so.

University of Arizona Professor Brent White argued in his paper "Underwater and Not Walking Away" [See 45 Wake Forest Law Review 971 (2010)] that people should consider cutting mortgage losses. He indicated that by 2009 over a third of Americans were underwater on their mortgage nationwide, with some areas like Merced and El Centro, California experiencing an 85% underwater rate, meaning 85% of homeowners owed more on their mortgages than the value of their homes. In certain states, known as non-recourse states (such as Alaska Arizona, California, Connecticut, Idaho, Minnesota, North Carolina, North Dakota,

Oregon, Texas, Utah, Washington State), there is even greater incentive to walk because the bank cannot come after the mortgage holder's other assets for the excess debt. They can only use the property to satisfy the mortgage debt. The state list cited is not exhaustive so please check the current law in your state.

If you choose to walk, be aware that it will impact your credit for at least two years. If you continue to pay your other bills faithfully, it's possible that you can purchase another home after the two years have passed. If you think you could not live with yourself if you walked away, then don't do it. "To thine own self be true," as Shakespeare said.

PART 2

Save for the Important, Invest in the Prudent

CHAPTER 6

Save, Save, Save

This Chapter explores issues associated with saving money. The advantages are many. People who save feel more secure. If an emergency arises, they know they can weather the storm without too much hardship. People who save can occasionally splurge. If they would like to treat themselves to a new television or an enjoyable experience, such as a concert or mini vacation, they can without putting themselves into debt.

Saving is not a new topic. It has been explored frequently and expeditiously. Sometimes we just need reminders of why we benefit from not spending every penny we make. Following this Chapter's tips will help you save, save, save.

Tip 1: Save Consistently

Much has been said of the old adage—pay yourself first—and that's because many benefits come from it. Making this happen is simple. Deposit your paycheck into your savings account first and then shift into your checking account what you need to pay your bills, plus a little extra for discretionary spending. Mentally, you will not think the saved amount is available to be easily spent because it is out of your line of financial sight.

Let's say your take-home pay amounts to $3000 per month, and you decide to save 10%. To do this, deposit the entire $3000 into savings and then shift $2700 into your checking account to pay your mortgage or rent, and other monthly expenses. Within a year, your savings account will build to $3600 plus interest. This gives you enough funds to pay for an additional month's worth of expenses plus emergencies, such as an unexpected car repair.

Further, you may have additional bills come due once every six months or once a year, such as car insurance, property taxes, or home owners insurance. Save for these expenses monthly by shifting even less into your checking account. If you want to save $600 per month so that you have the resources to cover these additional expenses, shift only $2400 into your checking account.

Saving consistently pays off in peace of mind because you know you have the resources to cover an emergency and the forthcoming annual and semi-annual payments.

Tip 2: Save the Extras

Depending on their talents, most people have multiple ways to earn extra money. Writers can produce extra magazine or web articles, musicians might take on special gigs, handymen might help neighbors paint their homes, and executives can receive bonuses. Bank the extra income in your savings or money market accounts. Among the worse mistakes individuals make is to treat bonuses as regular income and buy homes and other items based on expected ongoing bonus income.

Bonuses, by their nature, can change yearly and even be suspended when companies encounter financial difficulties. Thus, bonuses should be spent on one-time costs. If your bonus will cover a fancy car or kitchen remodel, then buy what you desire, but do not pay for such items with loans that require ongoing bonus income to pay off.

Other unexpected resources may flow your way, such as rebate checks from federal or state governments. Save these as well. If you receive an unexpected gift from a relative, place it in savings. Even loose change found on the street should go into a piggy bank.

Money is available everywhere you look. I once found a $20 bill while walking. Wily Writer, a freelancer in her eighties, found a $20 bill inside the pocket of a shirt she bought at a consignment store. She missed it when initially purchasing the item and found a pleasant surprise in her closet.

Don't be too proud to pick up a penny. Ten add up to a dime and ten dimes equal a dollar. Make it a game to see how much money you have by the end of the year from found money. Some banks and credit unions have machines that quickly count change and give you a slip for the total amount to be refunded by a teller.

Tip 3: Become Your Own Bailout Plan

Prior to the rapid rise in the economy between 2004 and 2006, the conventional wisdom was that everyone should have at least six months of savings to weather a downturn. During that giddy period when jobs were plentiful and it was easy to change, some pundits lowered their recommendations to three months of savings. The recession began in December 2007. During the ensuing years, some individuals were unemployed for over 11 months. This indicates you need at least a year's worth of savings in your emergency account.

The federal government bails out individuals with unemployment checks. These payments are modest amounts to help individuals weather a storm, usually for six months, although sometimes the benefits have been extended for a year, 99 weeks, or more.

The reality is you must plan for difficult times during periods of abundance. That's why it's best to sock away a year's worth of expenses while gainfully employed.

By the time most people start receiving unemployment checks, they are barely scraping by. With substantial savings accumulated during periods of abundance, you can bail out your own finances. That way you do not have to depend on the slow winding ways of Washington or state government to keep solvent. Better to be self-reliant and float your own financial boat.

Tip 4: Look for Higher Interest Rates

Is your money market fund paying 0.03% interest or less? Obtain rate sheets from your bank and transfer money into higher interest certificate of deposit (CD) accounts. Do a search of banks on the Internet and consider transferring money to banks that pay more interest. As long as the bank is insured by the Federal Deposit Insurance Corporation (FDIC), then your money is safe and will be backed by the federal government up to $250,000 in the event that the bank defaults. On its website, www.fdic.gov, the FDIC says, "Since the FDIC was established in 1933, no depositor has ever lost a single penny of FDIC-insured funds. FDIC insurance covers all deposit accounts, including checking and savings accounts, money market deposit accounts and certificates of deposit. FDIC insurance does not cover other financial products and services that banks may offer, such as stocks, bonds, mutual fund shares, life insurance policies, annuities or securities."

Consider bond mutual funds. These funds may pay more than CD accounts. Look at the historic return rates, both at the last month, last year, and last 10 years. You can acquire a prospectus to see how the fund has been diversified.

High quality municipal bond funds can also save you money, particularly if they pay a guaranteed interest rate that is not taxed.

Tip 5: Consider Automatic Investing in a Stock Account

Some people fear the stock market, and rightly so. It can lose 1000 points in a day, as it did on May 6, 2010, or gain 700 points in a day, as it also did the same day for a net loss of 300 points. Many people who saw their 401(k) plummet during the 2000 or 2007-2008 downturns vowed to get out and never return.

Long-term success in the market can come from dollar-cost averaging whereby busy individuals like Dedicated Doctor and Scattered Secretary can invest a certain amount in solid companies or mutual funds on a steady basis. You thus buy into both down and up markets, but on average you will most likely make money in the long term. If you plan to stay in ten, twenty, or thirty years, then you will not worry too much when the market takes a plunge or celebrate too fiercely when the market accelerates like a rocket. Choose a fund management company to invest for you, but be sure to scrutinize their management costs. These companies take care of creating the fund and handling the transaction costs. You can thus relax and not become too bothered.

Tip 6: Return Items You Do Not Use

Often times, individuals buy items that they do not need or do not use. The items gather dust in closets, cupboards, or garages. This is a useless waste of your money. If an item hasn't been used in a month after purchase, return it. Some stores will let you return new items ninety or 180 days after purchase. Save all receipts in a drawer or tape the receipt to the item after you buy it. This makes the receipts easier to find for returns.

Plop the recovered money into your piggy bank or in an envelope to be spent on something more useful later. There are times when you purchase items or services and they do not live up to your expectations. Do not sit and steam about it. Instead, ask for your money back. While you may not obtain everything sought, you are guaranteed to receive nothing if you do not write, call, or email the offending company. Many large companies have customer service sections to deal with complaints, and they know it pays in the long run to keep their customers happy.

Tip 7: If the Investment Sounds Too Good to Be True, Pass

A colleague of Learned Lawyer's lost $350,000, his entire life savings, on a good deal. He had invested his retirement income and his daughters' college funds in what turned out to be a Ponzi scheme. It's all gone and he's depressed.

Unfortunately shysters who look to rob people like Learned Lawyer's colleague with Ponzi schemes are a dime a dozen. They particularly prey on busy professionals and the elderly. Named after Charles Ponzi, who duped thousands of New England residents into investing in postage stamp speculation in the 1920s, the U.S. Securities and Exchange Commission defines a Ponzi scheme as "investment fraud that involves the payment of purported returns to existing investors from funds contributed by new investors." Ponzi schemes usually offer guaranteed returns of 10% or more, which sounds great when banks are offering 0.3% interest on savings. Rarely can anyone truly guarantee high rates of return on investments. It's not an investment if the return is assured because by their nature investments carry risks.

If you get offered such an investment, run. These are the Bernie Madoff-type schemes. While these may pay well for those who enter first and get out early, even they do not escape free as they may be subject to "claw backs," or legal rules which permit other investors to sue them for their gains. Because early investors were paid off with later investors' money, later investors argue that they should be able to recoup at least part of their losses from the early investors.

This happened to Dedicated Doctor and his wife who invested over $400,000 in a "guaranteed" real estate fund run by New Mexico real estate entrepreneur Doug Vaughan. As early investors, they were repaid their initial $400,000 as interests. When sued, the bankruptcy trustee sought more than their net gains; she wanted their principal. Dedicated Doctor's wife was so devastated by the loss that she soon developed cancer on her face and had to have several skin cancer removing surgeries.

The reality is that all associated with Ponzi schemes lose, and when they collapse the stress can be immense. Victims can sue perpetrators, but they will be lucky to recover pennies on the dollars because most perpetrators use the scheme to fund elaborate lifestyles for themselves. While homes, boats, and personal effects can be sold at auctions, the recovered funds are usually a small fraction of what the perpetrator paid for the items. The money they paid for services, such as salaries for maids, housekeepers, and chauffeurs, is completely lost.

Sending fraud perpetrators like Madoff and Vaughan to jail yields a measure of satisfaction to the victims and society benefits by keeping them from defrauding others. Nevertheless, the victims cannot be made whole from the financial and emotional harm.

Victims should correct their prior tax returns to eliminate the profits they paid taxes on, but which turned out to be illusory.

Learned Lawyer's colleague recouped $50,000 from the IRS after he filed corrected tax returns to eliminate the false gains.

Further, avoid email fraud. You know the ones beginning with "Dearest," "Hun" or "Beloved." They ask for an investment to help liberate a gold mine in Nigeria or to probate the will of a rich ancestor in England. Immediately hit the delete button. They arrive in your in-box designated as spam for a reason. Get-rich-quick schemes often leave victims much poorer.

* * *

The bottom line is to relish opportunities to save money the old fashioned way. You'll feel better about your life and more appreciative of your money when you accumulate it one dollar at a time.

CHAPTER 7

Creative Estate Matters

What do Abraham Lincoln, Howard Hughes, and James Dean have in common? If you guessed that all three souls departed earth without wills, you would be right. They are not unlike most Americans. In any given year approximately 60%–75% perish without leaving written plans for distributing their estates. The reasons for the reluctance to do so vary. Many are unwilling to confront the concept of mortality. If they don't make a will, they won't die. Others think that writing a will may hasten their ascension to Heaven, or increase the numbers longing for their departure. Still others are just lazy. Some think it will cost too much.

No matter the excuse, there is only one good reason to not have a will: you like your state's method for dividing your estate. Thus, this Chapter encourages you to know your state's plans for your assets after you ascend to those colorful gardens in the sky. If you do not like the results, then you must prepare your estate division in advance to give yourself peace of mind. The expense to your family could be enormous if you do not plan ahead. By reading this book and adopting its tips, you have saved a lot of money. The last thing you'd want to do is have your savings go to the wrong person once you've made your last withdrawal.

Wills, trusts, and powers of attorneys are for the living. They help your survivors divide your assets in a systematic fashion and lessen their stress. Once the documents are complete, if events cause your life to expire suddenly, pre-planning means you took care of your family, friends, animals, and charities.

Tip 1: Know Your State's Estate Plan

States craft laws, known as intestacy statutes, to give the deceased person's assets to the closest relatives in the blood lines. Family trees differ. A person may be single like Lively Lawyer, married like Dedicated Doctor, or divorced like Seattle Businessman. A person may also possess surviving children, parents, grandparents, siblings and other descendants. Some individuals come from small families where they were the only child and their parents were also only children. This tree is illustrated in Table 8-1.

Table 8-1
Grandfather - Grandmother   Grandfather - Grandmother
\   /
Mother   -   Father
/
Only Child

Should Only Child in Table 8-1 die, leaving behind just his parents, his estate would go to both of them equally. If Only Child likes the outcome, then there is no need for a will. If, however, the person would prefer to disinherit one parent or change the split from 50-50 to 80-20 or something else, then he needs a will. Similarly, if the person wants to leave items to friends, he must do so by will.

A person can tell a parent to give all clothes to her best friend, but unless mandated in a will, the parent would have no legal obligation to do so.

Table 8-2				
	Wife	-	Husband	
	/	/	\	
Child 1		Child 2		Child 3

If a family looks like that in Table 8-2, then most intestate succession statutes will give Wife's assets to the surviving Husband expecting him to care for the children were she to predecease him. In some states, the situation can become more complicated if either married person has children from other relationships. Thus you have to look up your state's intestate succession statute to determine how it mandates distribution along blood lines. On your state's website, if you search the term "intestate succession," that should show you what you most need to know. Even if you hire an attorney to assist you, which I highly recommend, it's helpful to educate yourself in advance.

Tip 2: Write a Will

To be eligible to write a formal will, you must be 18 years of age, be of sound mind, understand the distribution you are making, and sign the written document at the end (also known as the foot) of the will in the presence of at least two witnesses (Louisiana requires three) who know they are signing a will. In about half the states, if you write the will entirely in your own handwriting, you can sign and date it without the need for witnesses.

There's no IQ requirement to write a will. Thus, the Forrest Gumps of the world can leave property to others. Nevertheless, you must be in your right mind to do so. Lawyers who know clients with lucid and not lucid moments have been known to videotape the will signing ceremony to provide later proof that the person was of sound mind when he signed the will.

The testamentary capacity (another phrase referring to "of sound mind") rarely becomes an issue unless someone does something a court finds unusual, such as the woman who declared her hatred for men and left all her money to the National Women's Party in the 1930s or the husband who thought his wife was having affairs with everyone in the neighborhood and wrote her out of his will. In both instances, courts overturned the will.

To start your will-making process, identify your property and beneficiaries. The three major categories of property are real estate (land and the buildings attached); personal property (cars, clothes, computers, furnishings, art work, watches, jewelry, personal papers, telephones and so forth); and intellectual or intangible property (trademarks, patents, and copyrights). Stocks, bonds and financial instruments are sometimes classified as inchoate or intangible property, but it's easier to think of them as personal property.

For example, let's assume that Wife mentioned in Table 8-2 is an author and owns the assets listed in Table 8-3:

Table 8-3	
Real Estate: a co-owned condo at	1 Avenue of the Americas #12F, New York, NY
Personal Property	2010 Honda Accord 2 watches (Rolex and Timex) Two closets full of clothes Furniture 5 paintings Laptop, iPad, Kindle Personal Bank Account with $30,000
Intellectual Property	Copyrights in 5 books

When Wife in Table 8-2 writes a will, she will think of likely beneficiaries such as her husband and three children, friends, and charities. Table 8-4 gives an example of what a simple will for her might look like. The will lists personal information, and names those to whom she wishes to leave the items she owns. Typically a person who is married may wish to leave all assets to a spouse, or divide the assets between the spouse and children, or leave friends something. These gifts need to be spelled out specifically as to who is to receive what item.

Notice that Wife gives away property belonging to her, and benefits those closest to her, namely family and friends, and a charity. In community property states (Arizona, California, Idaho, Louisiana, Nevada, New Mexico, Texas, and Washington), marriage is treated as a partnership in which each spouse has control over 50% of the assets. Thus, a spouse can only leave her share of a house owned in community property to another. She could not give away the entire house. In Table 8-4, Wife left her share of the home to her spouse. She would have potentially created an awkward situation if she had left her share to someone other than Husband, such as Child 1 who wants to sell immediately. Couples who live together should discuss such issues in advance so there are no surprises once one of them ascends to the great beyond.

Table 8-4. Last Will and Testament of Wife

I, Wife, a resident of city, county, and state of New York, hereby make this Will and revoke all prior Wills and Codicils.

I. PERSONAL INFORMATION

I was born on January 1, 1950 in New York, New York. I am married to Husband, who I will refer to as "my spouse". We were married on February 1, 1976 in New York, NY. We have three children: Child 1, born on March 1, 1978, Child 2, born on April 1, 1980, and Child 3, born on March 1, 1982.

II. GIFTS

I hereby give my property to the following persons:

To my spouse, I leave my share of our home and its furnishings, my share of our joint bank account, and my residuary estate, that is any gifts not specifically given to another individual.

To Child 1, I leave my car; to Child 2, I leave my watches and clothing; and to Child 3, I leave my laptop, iPad, and Kindle.

I leave the copyrights in my books in trust to Writers Organization, a charity, to use royalties to buy computers for high school seniors who receive a 3.5 GPA or higher in English.

To members of my Writers Critique Group who were named in the acknowledgements to my latest book, I leave my books on writing. They can pick in the order they joined the group.

If any beneficiary under this Will does not survive me by 30 days, then I shall be deemed to have survived such person and their share falls into my residuary estate.

III. PERSONAL REPRESENTATIVE OR EXECUTOR

I appoint my Spouse as Executor of my Will. If he is unable or unwilling to serve, I name Child 1 as alternate Executor. My Executor and alternate shall have all powers granted by applicable laws of New York to carry out all provisions of this Will, may use provisions and procedures for the simplified handling of estates, may hold in trust the share of any minor beneficiary until s/he reaches age 18, and shall not be required to post a bond.

I, Wife, hereby sign this Will in New York, NY on this 1 day of January, 2014.

*Wife*________________ [signature]

Wife________________ [Printed Name]

IV. WITNESSES

Each of us hereby states, under penalties of perjury, that on 1 January, 2014, in New York, NY, we observed Wife declare the above document to be her last will and testament. She then asked us to serve as her witnesses and signed the document in our presence. She appeared to be of sound mind, acting of her own free will, and not under any force or duress. We are signing our names in her presence and in the presence of each other.

_____*Calvin A*_____	_____*Darrell B*_____
Signature of Witness #1	Signature of Witness #2
Calvin A, 2 First Avenue, NY, NY	Darrell B, 3 Second Avenue, NY, NY
Printed name and address of Witness #1	Printed name and address of Witness #2

Two witnesses signed the will in Table 8-4, but it was not notarized. Only Louisiana requires a notary, although some lawyers will have the will notarized as a matter of formality.

Wife left her residuary estate and her share of their joint bank account to Husband. The residuary refers to what remains after all other specified gifts have been given to the intended recipients. This is an important clause because money could flow into the estate after death, such as from a judgment or the settlement of a wrongful death action against someone who caused the untimely departure. The most prominent example is the Goldman family's successful lawsuit to hold O.J. Simpson accountable for Ron Goldman's death. With no residuary clause, the after-death income gets divided according to the state's laws of intestate succession.

Joint bank accounts are often setup with rights of survivorship so that the money will transfer automatically to the survivor once he or she presents a death certificate. Most banks, insurance companies, pension plans, and so forth will often ask the account holder to designate payable on death (POD) recipients. These accounts then do not become part of the estate.

In Table 8-4, Wife also benefited members of her writing critique group. To leave gifts to those who are not related by blood, you must do so by writing either in a will or a memorandum that is referenced in the will. Simply state you left a memorandum that details specific gifts to friends. Under the Uniform Probate Code, you can keep changing this memorandum until that mysterious date when you can write no more.

Further, property must be left to human beings. A California woman left half of her estate to Roxy Russell, who turned out to be a dog. Animals cannot inherit property. They can, however, be beneficiaries of trusts created to support them during their lives as explained in the next tip.

Tip 3: Create Trusts to Handle Special Circumstances

Trusts can be activated while you are living (known as *inter vivos* trusts) or created in a will (testamentary trusts). Trusts often involve particular language. A settlor or grantor is the person who creates the trust. A trustee becomes the legal owner of trust assets and is responsible for their management. The beneficiaries will hold equitable title in the trust and receive its benefits. A trust, thus, divides a normal title to property between a trustee (legal owner) and a beneficiary (equitable owner). If the trustee and the beneficiary are the same, the divided title will merge to create one title and end the trust. The *res* (pronounced rāz and not to be confused with the Rez, which is a nickname for an Indian reservation) is the trust property. A trust must be settled with at least $1, with other assets to be added later, such as from the settlor's will or a bank account with the trust as the payable on death (POD) designee. With no trust property, there is no trust. And there must be a purpose, the reason the trust was created, and the trustee must be given duties. Trusts do not have to be witnessed. They should, however, be notarized.

In Table 8-4, Wife left "the copyrights in my books in trust to Writers Organization, a charity, to use royalties to buy computers for high school seniors who receive a 3.5 GPA or higher in English." Wife is the settlor of the trust. The *res* is the copyrights in her books, which may generate royalty income through print, audio, and e-book sales and the exploitation of film, television and other rights. The trustee is Writers Organization, which has the duty to buy and distribute computers to the beneficiaries, who are high school seniors with a 3.5 GPA or higher in English. As the trustee, Writers Organization has a duty to earmark the funds, that is separate them into a special account so it is clear what is trust money and how it was spent.

To create a simple trust for the care of a beloved pet, for example, the settlor could give $10,000 from her estate and her pet (the *res*) to a friend or bank (trustee) to care for the pet (beneficiary). If the bank is the trustee, it will most likely put a chip in the animal so that when it dies, the trust ends. Some people who stay in a mansion while caring for a pet have been known to purchase look-alike replacements to keep their benefit going after the original pet dies. The pet trust should specify who should receive any remaining funds after the pet's demise. Note that a pet and money can be left to the friend as in Table 8-5.

Table 8-5. Sample Trust for Care of Pet

I, Wife, a resident of New York, NY, hereby create this trust for the care of Poodle, my beloved pet of 7 years.

I. Trust

A. *Trust Property:* I hereby create this trust with $10,000 to be held in Good Bank, New York, NY. I also designate Poodle as trust property.

B. *Trustee:* My friend Judy Avila has agreed to serve as Trustee. She is to hold $10,000 in trust for the care of Poodle, including feeding, grooming, and vet care. If Judy Avila should predecease Poodle, I designate Phil Jackson as successor trustee.

C. *Beneficiary:* Judy Avila and Poodle will benefit from this trust.

D. *Trust Purposes*: Judy Avila is to use the money for the care of Poodle while it lives. If any money remains after Poodle dies from natural causes, then Judy Avila may use it for whatever purpose she desires.

____Wife_____, 1/1/2014

Wife, 1 American Avenue #12F, New York, NY

Trusts can become complicated when there are millions of dollars involved. In her fourteen-page will, hotel queen Leona

Helmsley left $12 million for the care of her dog Trouble, who was to continue to live in her mansion. A court later reduced the amount to $2 million, finding $12 million to be excessive, and added the difference to her charitable trust. Helmsley left her chauffeur $100,000 and two grandchildren nothing "for reasons which are known to them."

More often, a trust is created for the care of an individual, such as a minor child or for charity. If the settlor wants to keep the beneficiary completely confidential, then the trust should be set up as a living trust, and completely funded during the settlor's life. Individuals with mistresses or secret lovers often choose this arrangement because wills become public documents when they are probated. The contents of a living trust can remain private forever. Trusts are presumed to be revocable (changeable), unless the settlor specifies they are irrevocable (not changeable).

Several decades ago, a deceased person left his residuary estate in trust for the benefit of his friends, with the only direction to his designated trustees: "You know who they are." The court overturned this gift to friends as too indefinite to create a private class of beneficiaries. Bottom line: friends must be identified by name. In Table 8-4, Wife specified that the members of her writing critique group were identified in her latest book. While the names were not mentioned in the document, they are easily ascertainable by looking at her latest book.

Setting up trusts can be complex and I urge you to seek legal advice. Sample trusts can be found on the web at various websites, such as www.freelegalforms.net, www.legalzoom.com, or www.USLegalForms.com. The financially literate will check out the free forms first and then move to the paid ones if the free ones prove inadequate.

Tip 4: Write a Power of Attorney

This document springs into existence in the event you become mentally or physically incapacitated and can no longer manage your financial and personal affairs. A Power of Attorney should be signed and witnessed. The person with a Power of Attorney may access your bank accounts to pay your bills, and they may also receive paychecks from your employer or a government agency for your benefit. Pick someone in whom you have complete confidence, be it a family member or a friend, who is not deeply in debt and does not have gambling or substance abuse issues. You do not want to recover from a medical emergency to find that someone gambled or snorted away your money.

The legal requirements for a Power of Attorney can vary from state to state. Thus you should check your state's website for samples.

To make the sample Power of Attorney in Table 8-6 effective, the holder must receive two notarized statements from qualified health care professionals, one of whom must be a doctor stating that you have become medically incapacitated and can no longer act for yourself.

Share with your Power of Attorney what you would like to happen in the event of a major catastrophe, such a heart attack, stroke, or accident that results in you being placed on life support. Do you want to receive hydration and nutrition? Do you want a machine to breathe for you? If so, for how long? If a doctor tells your attorney in fact that you are unlikely to return to consciousness, do you want to have the breathing machines immediately disconnected or do you want time? If so, how much time? A week? A month? A year? Better yet is to create a Living Will that gives detailed instructions to assist the holder of your Power of Attorney.

Table 8-6. Power of Attorney

I, Wife, reside at 1 Avenue of the Americas #12F, New York, NY.

I appoint Husband, who also resides at 1 Avenue of the Americas #12F, New York, NY to serve as my attorney-in-fact. If Husband is unable to serve, then I appoint Child 1 to serve as successor attorney-in-fact.

This power of attorney shall become effective only if I become incapacitated and will terminate upon my recovery from illness or upon my death. I can revoke it prior to my death at any time. My attorney-in-fact shall obtain notarized statements from two qualified health care professionals, one of whom shall be a physician, as to my incapacity. By incapacity I mean that I am unable to effectively manage my personal care, property or financial affairs.

I intend by this power of attorney to avoid a court-supervised guardianship or conservatorship. Should my attempt be defeated, I ask that my Husband or Child 1 be appointed as guardian or conservator of my person or estate.

During my incapacity, my attorney-in-fact shall have the power to act in my name, place and stead in any way which I myself could do with respect to the following activities to the extent permitted by law: real estate transactions; stock and bond transactions; commodity and option transactions; tangible personal property transactions; banking and other financial institution transactions; business operating transactions; insurance and annuity transactions, estate, trust and other beneficiary transactions; claims and litigation; personal and family maintenance, securing benefits from Social Security, Medicare, Medicaid or other government programs or civil or military service; retirement plan transactions; tax matters, including any transactions with the Internal Revenue Service; decisions regarding lifesaving and life prolonging medical treatment; decisions relating to medical treatment, surgical treatment, nursing care, medication, hospitalization, institutionalization in a nursing home or other facility and home health care; and transfer of property or income as a gift to others for the purpose of qualifying me for governmental medical assistance.

I agree that any third party who receives a copy of this power of attorney may act upon it.

________*Wife, 1/1/2014*_____________

Wife, 1 American Avenue #12F, New York, NY.

STATE OF New York)

) ss.

COUNTY OF County

The foregoing instrument was acknowledged before me on 1/1/2014

____.

Notary Public

My Commission Expires: ________________________

(seal)

These are difficult questions and will require some thought. A Belgian man emerged from a coma after being locked in for 23 years. He could hear everything around him but was unable to communicate. The victim of a motorcycle accident awoke after 19 years in a coma. A brain scan revealed that his brain had built new neural pathways around previously damaged tissue. As science continues to advance, eventually doctors will be able to advise caregivers with more certainty as to whether a person is locked in or has truly left his body.

Tip 5: Powers of Attorney Are Good for Finances

Powers of Attorney save time and money. When my brother suffered a cardiac arrest, lost oxygen to the brain for approximately 28 minutes and was revived, he went into a coma and was unable to manage his affairs. He did not have a Power of Attorney. To manage his health care and financial issues, I had to obtain legal guardianship and conservatorship over him through the court system. As his guardian, I became responsible for managing his personal affairs, including dealing with doctors, nurses, case managers, and dietitians. As his conservator, I managed his assets, including qualifying him for Social Security disability insurance.

A Power of Attorney would have saved legal costs. I hired an attorney in my brother's home state. The court costs exceeded $1,200 and I paid an additional $2,500 for legal services. The attorney I hired billed in six minute increments, meaning every time she read an email or took a call from me, I was charged $22.50, even if the email was two lines and the phone message I left was 30 seconds long. These costs can add up quickly.

Tip 6: Guardianships Can Be Complicated

If you are short on cash and are applying to become a guardian in the state in which you live, try filling out a guardianship/conservatorship application yourself with the kits the courts provide. Another option for those with limited financial resources is to contact a law school clinic connected to a university near you. They may be able to file the paperwork for you or supervise your filling out the application. Better yet is to encourage loved ones to create a Power of Attorney. And write one for yourself as well.

In situations where the person is of means, several people may want to serve as guardian and conservator. A case involving multiple individuals seeking the roles concerned socialite Brooke Astor. The New York Supreme Court appointed Annette de la Renta guardian and JP Morgan Chase & Co. conservator in charge of her financial affairs. By the time Brooke Astor died at age 105 in 2007, she had executed more than 30 different wills and codicils over a period of 50 years. Several lawsuits were filed with people seeking to probate different wills. Ultimately, in 2012, all the parties reached a global settlement accepted by the Judge.

This Chapter laid out the core of these matters. I co-wrote the current version of *Wills and Trusts in a Nutshell* with Robert Mennell, which provides more details. Do not hesitate to hire an attorney. Seek a flat fee attorney to contain your costs. Preparing ahead will lower your stress and improve your life and make the lives of those left behind a little easier during difficult emotional times. Financial well-being can be shared with others through estate planning. Make sure your gifts go to those you want to benefit from your life-long accumulation.

PART 3

Navigating Life's Challenges

CHAPTER 8

Downsizing

Downsizing can take many forms. It can be voluntary as when a person retires, or involuntary as when he or she loses a job. A person may be furloughed, losing both hours and income. Some lose bonuses they had come to depend on when their company experiences a decline in revenue. Others must shift from a house to an apartment because they can no longer afford the payments or, due to aging or poor health, lack the physical strength to maintain their current space. This form of physical downsizing may mean giving up prized possessions and associated memories.

Downsizing in all its forms represents a shift from what *was* to what *is*. It requires adjusting to a new set of conditions. It can present a substantial change in work situations from leaving the house every day at a certain time to becoming house-bound. Here are several tips to help maintain financial well-being if you are downsized.

Tip 1: Adopt a Positive Attitude

After a drastic change in circumstances, an easy out might be to hold a pity party and spend days, weeks, even months or years in "woe is me" mode. Complaining and feeling sorry for yourself can lead to depression. Some folks park themselves in front of the television, watching soap operas, sports, or reality TV. Others stop bathing and changing clothes because they no longer have to go to work. These choices lead to deeper stages of despair.

Instead, face reality. Your situation will not improve while you sit in your pajamas playing video games. Rather, immediately make an attitude adjustment.

If you must get the anger out of your system, set a kitchen timer for 20 minutes to scream it out. If you need to cry, set the timer for 40 minutes. When the timer goes off, stop screaming or dry your eyes. Move on. Begin to think positively by accepting the situation as it is and inquiring as to what can be done now, at this moment, under the new state of affairs.

Ask yourself, "What is the best thing that has happened because of the downsizing?" Dr. Irene Blea went from earning $6000 a month as a tenured professor and department chair at Cal State Los Angeles to pulling in $800 a month after she lost her job following a freak accident that caused her to become disabled. She admits experiencing "profound intense, unending razor sharp grief" following the demise of her professional career plan, and the accompanying decline of her social life, love life, and income. She says her dream had been to move to New Mexico and write fulltime. "It finally hit me that I was angry at the conditions, complaining about my aches and pains. Yet here I was fulfilling my dream." She published on the Internet and sold her first historical novel *Susanna*, a portrayal of Hispanic females married off at ages 13, 14, and 15 to older men.

Look on the bright side, and grasp that the new reality brings fresh possibilities. The only thing that is guaranteed is that things will change so embrace the shift.

Tip 2: Be Open to the Possibilities

Are there things you always wanted to do, but never had the time? Downsizing brings moments to do the things you want to do. Ask yourself, "Do I like my career?" If so, sharpen your skills by taking more classes. If not, take classes to train for a different career. If you have envisioned switching careers, explore what's available by doing research on the Internet or at the library.

Did you bemoan weight gain while performing your high stress job? Now you have hours to become fit by walking or biking in your neighborhood or exercising at your favorite gym. Do pushups and sit-ups to build arm strength and check out a yoga or fitness DVD from the library to improve flexibility, conditioning, and breathing capacity.

In the past, did you miss many of your kids' or grandkid's important events? Now you can spend entire days with them. Downsizing increases chances to hang out with family, friends, neighbors, and opportunities to improve your community through volunteering. Take advantage. You never know when the next high-stress job might be right around the corner. Sometimes volunteering can lead to a steady job. You get to practice old skills and add new ones.

Let your spouse and children know how much you love them and reassure them that your job loss is temporary. A study at the University of California at Davis determined that children were 15 percent more likely to repeat a grade when the head of household lost a job.[1] Another study by a University of Chicago professor found that "adolescent children of lower income single mothers

---

[1] Michael Luo, "Recession Exacts an Emotional Toll on Children," *N.Y. Times*, Nov. 12, 2009.

had an increased chance of dropping out of school and showed declines of emotional well-being."[2]

These studies are further reminders that being downsized is not the time to engage in pity parties. If, on the one hand, your family observes you looking for a job, building new skills through volunteering, or going back to school to retrain, they may feel less worried about the future. If, on the other hand, they see you lying around, watching television or surfing the Internet as the house grows more unkempt, then they will become frightened. Loved ones depend on you, and they adjust as you adjust. If you handle the change in a positive manner, it will help them stay focused and feel emotionally secure. Take on more chores, particularly if the other spouse has become the sole breadwinner. Have dinner waiting when he or she walks through the door. This shows you care and are willing to contribute labor when you cannot add financially to the family's well-being.

Tip 3: Explore Your Entrepreneurial Spirit

Some individuals were born entrepreneurs. These individuals were selling lemonade at age five and performing plays and charging admission by age seven. Some of these early business people went on to build successful enterprises. Others listened to the voices of wizened elders who advised them to take steady day jobs. For a while that worked, but then they found themselves downsized and started to wonder what might have been.

If you are one of these individuals, then losing a job might present a golden opportunity to tap into an entrepreneurial spirit that has lain dormant for too long. If your dream was to start an Internet business, now may be the time to do so. You can start by selling things on eBay that you no longer use. If your aspiration is

[2] *Id.*

to write, like Dr. Irene Blea, go to the computer, turn it on, open up a file, and type "The Beginning." These two words can jumpstart the novel that you have been plotting in your head for years or a nonfiction article based on your field of expertise. For example in one month, Wily Writer wrote a novel containing the bare bones of a good story although it was not of publishable quality given that her character names kept changing midstream.

No matter the dream, ask yourself, "What do I have to offer that others would want to pay for? What might others need that I can uniquely fill? Is there a demand for the product or service I want to sell? Who might purchase this product or service? How will I reach them?"

In answering these questions, take a page from Dale Carnegie's magnificent book *How to Win Friends and Influence People*, and think in terms of other people's interests. If your answer to the first question is "I'm a hard worker and I'm detail oriented," then entrepreneurship may *not* be for you. That's an answer from someone who wants to work for others.

Entrepreneurs have to be big-picture thinkers. Bill Gates did not build Microsoft by advertising himself as a hard worker, even though he is one. Rather, he foresaw the need for software to accompany the computer age and became a multi-billionaire by filling an unmet need.

If you have something to offer that others might need and you know how to reach your target audience, then starting your own business may be the way to go. Downsizing may become the impetus spurring you to fulfill a long-held desire.

Tip 4: You Must Do Something

Whether a person voluntarily retires from a job or is laid off, the person must find something to do. Human beings are not meant to be sedentary. Lie in bed for a day and notice how your muscles start to atrophy. Stop reading and observe how your brain does not function at optimum capacity. "Use it or lose it" is a phrase that applies to much of the human condition.

Scott Lovering retired after he sold his business for several million dollars. He became quickly bored and took odd jobs to keep busy. One of them was playing an extra in movies. Although he didn't need the funds, he was paid over $2000 for sixteen days of long hours on the set of *Terminator Salvation*. Lovering says, "I didn't do it for the money. I was looking for something fun to do. I put up with the long hours to see myself immortalized in celluloid on the silver screen." Unfortunately for Lovering, that didn't happen. Scenes containing his image were eliminated by editors. He told me, "I didn't see myself, but one person said he thought he saw me walk by Christian Bale. I plan to buy the DVD to see if I can find that scene. Then I'm going to email everyone and tell them to freeze a particular frame to find me."

Even though Lovering's goal didn't exactly pan out, he received the benefit of something fun to do and he got paid.

In searching for a job, designate a time for that activity and do it religiously either at home, the library or by going on interviews. Be committed to the search.

Find friends who have time available to go to the movies or other events. Film tickets cost less for afternoon matinees or at dollar theaters. Discount tickets may also be available through warehouses like Costco or Sam's Club. By volunteering to usher at musical and theatrical events, you can see them for free.

Avoid acquaintances who are depressed about their situations as their attitude can bring you down. Find those who are embracing their time off to relax, get in shape, learn new skills, or just have fun.

Tip 5: Adopt a New Budget to Fit the Current Reality

As you accept the situation as it is, rethink your current budget and spending patterns. You have less money coming in, so even less should be going out. If your income loss was as drastic as Dr. Irene Blea's, you may need to seek some form of public assistance to get you over the hump. Before obtaining her education, Blea had been a single mother on welfare receiving food stamps. She said, "After all those years of climbing out, I couldn't believe that I was back where I started."

Sometimes individuals have to acknowledge that it is their turn to stand in line and acquire the benefits they long paid taxes for others to receive. Accept this as merely a bump on the road to ultimate happiness.

One of the hardest adjustments may be to draft a budget. Like the one mentioned in *Chapter 3: Spending Frugally*, you must indicate current income and spending commitments. Ask yourself, "What is a need and what is a want?" Spending over two hundred fifty dollars a month to obtain 500 television channels and special events may feel like a necessity for some, but it is indeed a luxury. Consider adjusting down to limited basic cable, which in some markets cost about $20 per month, or cut cable altogether. Go to a retail store and buy a digital antenna to pick up all the free channels available in your area. Experience plenty of entertainment on the networks, which offer comedies, dramas, game shows, and reality TV.

Next, reevaluate your cell phone plan. Maybe you needed a $100 monthly plan for its data connections when you had clients requiring immediate attention. But if the clients have gone, so should the plan. Consider switching to prepaid where you pay a certain amount, about ten cents per minute as you use the service, or a flat $30 to $50 monthly fee.

Were you eating out once or more per day? Now is the time to grocery shop and cook your own food. You can eat healthier by buying primarily foods like fruits, vegetables, beans, rice, poultry, fish and beef in the grocery and preparing meals yourself. If you don't cook, check out *The Joy of Cooking* or Julia Child's *Mastering the Art of French Cooking* from the library and experiment. This could be the beginning of a love affair between you and food. Julia Child took up cooking as a housewife in France when she had a lot of time on her hands. For her, food preparation became art and avocation.

While at the grocery, buy vitamins to help maintain optimum health and cut down on doctor visits. Bestselling authors Dr. Daniel Amen and Dr. Mark Hyman both recommend taking a daily multivitamin and omega supplements. Similarly, brush and floss your teeth after every meal to decrease needs for a dentist. Spend money for hygiene cleaning that maintains dental health.

Rethink your housing costs. Can you afford to pay your mortgage or rent? If not, you need to explore selling or renting your home, or seeking a release from your rental agreement. Although it may not be comfortable, consider shared housing arrangements with friends and relatives. If you're willing to live with strangers, search advertisements either online at a website like www.craigslist.com or in newspapers for those with rooms to rent. If you do move in with someone, prepare to obey their rules to increase the possibility of peaceful coexistence. If you are willing to rent to strangers, investigate their background. My great aunt Callie would visit potential tenants' current location before agreeing to rent to them. She was searching for good tenants, and neighbors.

If you can continue to live in your current space, coldly appraise your maintenance costs. Can you take over the cleaning, gardening and repair of your home? I did these activities before the economic downturn because I like working with my hands. I took a course in basic home repair through Continuing Education and learned to determine when to use a screw versus a nail to hold things together. Your house becomes a home as you care for it. By repairing those items within your competence, you save money and obtain exercise.

Should your mortgage become unaffordable, consider selling or renegotiating your mortgage terms with the bank. The economic downturn created so many distressed properties that banks are not eager to take back real estate because they become responsible for maintaining the space.

Tip 6: Clear Your Clutter

You may have papers piled up in the garage, clothes hanging in a closet that have not been worn in decades, and other no longer used items scattered throughout the house. As articles gather dust, they could affect your breathing. Now is the moment to let go. Trim down your home as you slim your body.

Published Poet had years of accumulation from her shopping expeditions. Forty percent of it had never been opened or consumed. Her one bedroom apartment overflowed with 150 pairs of shoes, a hundred boxes of crayons, notebooks, and clothes, unopened boxes containing patio furniture, newspapers, magazines and books. After her bedroom became full, she began sleeping on her couch. Her daughter packed up Published Poet's things and moved her to another city. During the cleaning, she gave away 80% of her mother's possessions. Published Poet never missed a single item. Likewise, you probably will not miss anything you sell on eBay and at garage sales, or donate to Goodwill, Salvation Army or a similar organization.

Chances are you have bought things and wondered why. Let go of the unnecessary and unused. One of the best books on this topic is Karen Kingston's *Clear Your Clutter with Feng Shui*. While you may initially borrow it from the library, this is the kind of book to own so you can mark up the parts you find most important. Keep this book close by to refer to when clutter starts piling up. Kingston explains why we keep clutter, and how to identify and clear it from home and work spaces, and remain clutter free.

Kingston asks readers to count the clear space on their desk. For example, most people only keep free an area the size of an 8-1/2 x 11-inch piece of paper. She urges readers to assess the impact on them. Piles on desks often represent disorder in minds. That is certainly true for me. I have found that I need a clean desk to write, and Kingston's book helps me maintain one.

When messes accumulate in my home, I frequently grab Kingston's book and open a page. After reading several pages or a chapter, I put the book down and start cleaning. I find once the clutter is gone, my mind clears and I can concentrate and resume my day with effortless ease.

Life flows smoothly once you clear the clutter from your home.

Tip 7: Think in Absolute Rather than Relative Terms

Bill Gates and Warren Buffet lost billions during the financial markets decline but they persist as billionaires. You may have lost thousands, if not hundreds of thousands, or millions. Time to reality check your accounts: How much do you have? Is it enough to live on?

During boom times, some Internet millionaires bought elaborate homes containing rooms they never entered or completely furnished. They spent $50,000 a week or more to maintain their lifestyles. The *New York Times* profiled James McAfee, in its August 21, 2009, issue as part of a front page article about the decline of the super-rich. Mr. McAfee who founded the anti-virus computer software company that bears his name, saw his wealth diminish from $100 million to $4 million and was selling his last home in New Mexico and auctioning off his furniture and belongings to pay bills. After reading the article, my first thought was *I bet he feels poor.*

The reality was McAfee remained not just a millionaire, but a multimillionaire. He still had more than enough to live on for the rest of his life. He moved to Belize and bought a mansion on the beach. In 2012, he was accused of killing his neighbor and jailed after an international manhunt. The Chicago Sun Times reported on 11 December 2012 that McAfee had sold his life story rights to Impact Future Media, a Montreal-based television production company.

Adjusting attitudes and spending habits can make a difference in surviving a downturn. Be grateful for what you have at the moment. It may be a different amount from what you had two years or two months ago. But it's still yours.

Tip 8: Stick to the Moral and Legal

While a small part of you might urge the buying of lottery tickets or visiting of casinos to improve your income, ignore that nudge. Lottery tickets and slot machines are sucker's bets. They take in far more money than they will ever pay out. If you must go to a casino, stick to the free bingo activities where you get the cards without having to pay for them and can potentially win $50 or $100. This way you get your gambling entertainment fix without having to pay anything. People who have become gambling addicts should stay away from casinos. They are like the alcoholic who can never purchase liquor again. Be wary of going to places that trigger addiction urges.

Also, do not get drawn into illegal schemes to make money. The HBO drama *Hung* featured a high school baseball coach who lost his uninsured house in a fire and decided to become a gigolo to make money to rebuild the structure. A female poet friend became his pimp and designated their business as "Happiness Consultants." While the show *Hung* was entertaining, it did not depict real life options for people in the baseball coach's situation. For example, he would have been better off razing the house and selling the land rather than risk going to jail for illegal activities.

Similarly the AMC show *Breaking Bad* featured a high school chemistry teacher who took up meth production after being diagnosed with lung cancer. While thousands of real Americans have manufactured meth in their homes or created mobile labs in their cars to make ends meet, this form of quick cash is not worth it. They risk blowing up their homes and vehicles. When caught, the prison sentence will be lengthy. Drug dealers hook others and ruin lives. If tempted, remember the Biblical proclamation: "What you reap, so shall you sow."

Nor is it worth it to become a consumer of meth or other illegal drugs. While they appear to provide opportunities to escape, they are performance inhibitors. Tennis star Andre Agassi found this out when he took meth in 1997. His career collapsed. The former number one tennis player in the world declined to number 141. He eventually quit meth and rebuilt his career.[3]

---

[3] Andre Agassi, *Open* (2009).

To be downsized can be awful, but it can also bring enormous opportunities if faced realistically. The goal is to adjust to the changing circumstances of your life in a legal and moral manner. Find the silver linings of downsizing and ride them to your next grand adventure.

CHAPTER 9

When Bankruptcy Is the Best Option

As mentioned in *Chapter 1: Credit Dodger No More*, if you reach a point after tabulating your debt that you cannot pay it and cover the necessities of life, bankruptcy may be your best option. Bankruptcy is not a process to enter into lightly. A lot of people, like Published Poet, feel shame when they realize they must declare bankruptcy and start again. After the enactment of the Bankruptcy Reorganization Act of 2005, debtors must attend two financial education classes, one before they declare bankruptcy and a second before a final decree is issued. The stories people tell might break your heart.

In one class, a twenty-something male said his father, who shares his name, had taken out credit cards in his name and run up a tremendous debt. The young man said he was considering changing his name once the process was completed. The financial literacy counselor encouraged him to pursue that option. Another individual cried as he spoke of losing his home of several decades after he took out home equity loans that he could no longer repay. Several people spoke of problems paying medical bills after a dire illness afflicted a member of the family. Even for those with insurance, the co-pays overwhelmed them as the bills kept arriving at a time when the family member was unable to work. Others experienced a job loss that wiped out their only means of support. Some individuals, like Published Poet, had become compulsive shoppers and finally had to face that they could no longer pay the bills after fees and interest charges tripled or quadrupled the original amounts. Whatever the reason, bankruptcy is an option people have a *right* to consider.

The following tips describe the process of discharging debt through Chapter 7 of the bankruptcy process. If you do not qualify for complete discharge, you may be forced to file under Chapter 13 for a reorganization of your debt, and arrange to pay some of your debts over three to five years. Chapter 13 is a more complicated process than Chapter 7, and it is definitely harder to get a discharge of debts if you don't pay. You do not get your bankruptcy discharged until you finish a payment plan. Many people never finish. An attorney can assist you in determining whether Chapters 7 or 13 best fit your situation.

Tip 1: If You Fear Bankruptcy, Consider the Alternative

Several countries were founded on the premise that people deserve a second chance. In the 16th, 17th and 18th centuries, England and other European states created debtors' prisons. If someone couldn't repay their debts, they were incarcerated. As prisons began overflowing with non-violent criminals, England shipped prisoners to Georgia in the United States and Tasmania in Australia. The debts could have been as small as owing a shopkeeper for a glove and the person as young as 13. They often never returned to their homeland and never saw their families again. When you consider the historical alternatives, bankruptcy is a civilized approached to dealing with people who cannot repay their debts. You have no need to fear exile.

Tip 2: Calculate How Much You Owe

In this book's Chapter 1, you were asked to calculate the amount of money you owe others. This is also a necessity for someone filing for bankruptcy. For a complete liquidation of debt, a person must prove that his or her debts exceed assets and cannot possibly be repaid. In this book's Chapter 1, Scattered Secretary had debts of $30,437 as indicated in Table 1-1. The family also had monthly take-home income of $4396.54 and could afford to make the minimum payments of $640 per month and start a debt reduction fund of $250.

What if, however, the family with the same debt consisted of an elderly person who relied solely on a Social Security payment of $627 per month to fund all living expenses? Table 9-1 depicts this scenario.

TABLE 9-1: Budget		
Item	*Amount*	*Balance*
Social Security Income	$627	$627
Rent (subsidized)	-$207	$420
Phone	-45	$375
Food/ Prescription Drugs	-300	$75
Miscellaneous Expenses	-75	$0

While some Social Security checks are even lower, as payments depend on how much the person has contributed to the system, with this budget, the elderly person pays rent of $207 for subsidized government housing, $45 for phone, $300 for food and prescription drugs, and miscellaneous expenses of $75. Even if the person devoted all the income to paying the minimum payments of $640 in Table 9-2, she would not have enough money to pay the debts. The debt is unmanageable.

Table 9-2: Debt			
Creditor Name	*Total Amount Owed*	*Minimum Payment*	*Due Date*
Charge Account #1	$237	$10	January 1
Visa Card #1	$5303	$110	January 21
MasterCard #1	$4702	$100	January 17
Catalogue #1	$732	$20	January 4
Charge Account #2	$358	$10	January 22
Visa #2	$7398	$150	January 18
MasterCard #2	$2351	$50	January 9
Diner's Club	$9356	$190	January 20
Totals	*$30,437*	*$640*	

You might ask how someone racks up such debt. It's easy when the banks and creditors do not cut off the card once the person gets in over his or her head. Rather, the banks elect to add late payment fees and no-payment fees, and increase the interest rate or credit line, or both.

Published Poet had one company tack on a Credit Line Increase Fee of $100. Essentially, the company increased her credit line and charged her for it without her approval. Her previous balance before this fee was $150.84. She paid $35. But with the additional fee and a finance charge of $3.39, her balance grew to $219.23. She became so discouraged that the prior $35 payment became her last to that company. The company's greed caused it to lose a paying customer.

Most credit cards start out with minimum payments of zero or $10. At that level, the person with debt in Table 9-2 could devote all the miscellaneous expense fund of $75.25 to minimum payments. As fees get added and minimum payments grow, however, it decreases the ability and desire of the person to pay.

The 2009 Credit Card Bill of Rights, which went into effect in February 2010, aimed to stop some of the more horrendous creditor practices. For example, it required credit card companies give forty-five days' notice before they increase an annual percentage rate (APR), fees, and finance charges. Also, creditors are now forbidden from increasing interest rates on existing balances unless specific conditions are met, such as the expiration of a promotional time period, or failure to pay during the grace period. Creditors are also now required to inform debtors how long it will take to pay off a balance if the debtor just sends in the minimum payment and how much additional interest they will incur.

For example, consider Table 9-3 where the debtor possessed a credit card balance of $3053.31 with a minimum payment due of $61 and an interest rate of 13.24%. By paying in full, the debtor erases the debt in one month and pays no interest. However, this debt would take 22 years to pay off and the person would pay an estimated total of $6186 if the debtor sent in the minimum payment. If the debtor paid $103 a month, it would take only three years to pay off the balance and the debtor would pay $3720, for a savings of $2466.00, assuming no further credit card charges.

Table 9-3: Credit Card Payment Options				
Balance	*Interest Rate*	*Payment*	*Time to pay off*	*Total paid*
\$3053.31	13.24%	\$3053.31	1 month	\$3053.31
\$3053.31	13.24%	\$103	3 years	\$3720
\$3053.31	13.24%	\$61	22 years	\$6186

Should the debtor miss the due date, however, he or she incurs a late penalty fee of \$39 and the interest rate is subject to increase to 29.99%. Paying minimums or missing payments just dig consumers deeper into debt. Reviewing this information on credit card statements helps debtors make informed decisions.

Tip 3: Debts Can Become Uncollectable

Charles Parnall, an attorney with the firm Feferman and Warren, whose website is www.nmconsumerwarriors.com, says, "Most people don't know that there's a statute of limitation on debt: six years for written contracts and four years on oral accounts. Some people prefer not to file for bankruptcy, and they can avoid doing so if the statute of limitations has passed." Statute of limitations refers to the end of the right to file a legal claim. If you have not paid anything on a credit card, which was opened with a signed contract, then the creditor loses the right to file a lawsuit against you or otherwise pursue the claim legally after six years. Be wary of paying even a small amount as it will reset the statute of limitations.

Creditors sometimes only surreptitiously inform debtors of their right not to pay. For example, they might hide the information in language like, "Because of the age of your debt, we will not sue you for it and we will not report it to any credit reporting agency." The reality is they do not have the right to sue or report the debt once it becomes uncollectable.

Parnall says the rules are set up by the Fair Debt Collection Practices Act, a federal law that places restrictions on how long third party debt collectors can contact a debtor or alleged debtor. "Debt collectors can't lie to consumers," says Parnall. "They can't say they will sue you if they have never sued and have no intention of suing." He recommends turning the tables and asking them questions, such as "Who are you? Who do you work for? Where do you work? What account number are you calling about? What is the amount of the original debt? When was the last payment made? What is your mailing address, phone number, and fax number?" All this is important information to collect and review with an attorney.

Tip 4: Stop the Harassment

Bill collectors sometimes call and harass individuals at home and on the job. They phone, text, email, and post letters. You may get fed up. You do not have to respond to every text, email, and letter.

Parnall counsels that you neither argue with creditors, nor let them call you names. If they have the wrong person or account number, then you do not owe that debt. Parnall says, "If you don't owe it, they can't tell you that you do. . . . They can't say they are going to garnish your wages if they do not have a court order or judgment against you."

Debt collectors are prohibited from making threats against debtors, such as "to put you in jail, put a lien against your home, take all your wages," says Parnall. "Nor can they pretend to be attorneys. Be prepared to catch something as 'We are calling from the legal department'." He cautions to be alert to empty threats and simply ask the caller, "Are you an attorney?" Debt collectors are not permitted to tell other people about your debt, such as family members, supervisors or work colleagues. Parnall says, "They can't tell teenagers to tell Mom if she doesn't pay your bills, you will be out on the streets."

There's also a time restriction from 8:00 a.m. to 9:00 p.m. during which they can call, not before 8:00 a.m. and not after 9:00 p.m. You can ask them to stop calling you at work by saying, "I am not allowed to discuss personal issues at work." If they call you at inappropriate times and make threats, save the messages. In some states, a lawyer can use this against them.

Consider seeking a lawyer after you have been contacted by creditors, and do not want to be harassed. An attorney may be able to recover his or her fees from creditors who disobey the laws under the Unfair or Deceptive Acts or Practices (UDAP). That's why it's important to keep a record of the time and content of the calls. After a lawyer agrees to represent you, cease all contact with creditors and simply refer them to your representative. If they contact you after receiving a letter from an attorney, the tables will be turned and they can be sued.

Tip 5: Hire a Lawyer

Some people choose to go it alone and prepare their own bankruptcy papers. Given the complications of the Chapter 7 and Chapter 13 processes, I do not recommend this approach. There are bankruptcy lawyers who charge a flat fee. Investigate the fees by calling their offices. If you cannot afford to hire a lawyer, seek free assistance by calling the State Bar, Legal Aid, or law schools where you live. Lawyers are required to do a certain amount of work *pro bono* (for free) each year. Many law schools have clinics where they train law students by having them work on the problems of real people.

If after determining you can pay an attorney, schedule appointments to see at least two. Often they will give a free initial consultation. Hire the one you feel will best represent your case. If the lawyer does not promptly return your calls, that's a bad sign. Some attorneys may even let you pay their fee over a period of time (four to six months). Most likely, they will insist that you pay their entire fee before they file so they do not become one of your unsecured creditors whose debt is dismissed in bankruptcy. The attorney will have you sign a representation letter that puts you on notice about your "ongoing obligation to provide information that is complete, accurate and truthful," as one such agreement reads. It further states, "You will also be required to completely and accurately disclose all your assets and liabilities in the documents filed to commence your case."[1]

The attorney will need the information contained in Table 9-4 that will be submitted to the bankruptcy court on your behalf.

Table 9-4. Bankruptcy Court Required Information	
1.	Copies of pay stubs for the last six (6) months.
2.	Copies of your last two (2) Federal and State income tax returns with W-2s included.
3.	Documentation verifying that contributions to a mandatory retirement or 401(k) plan are indeed *mandatory*.
4.	Copies of current insurance billing showing coverage and premiums on all *owned* vehicles and real property.
5.	Copies of any lawsuit information.

1 Moore, Berkson & Gandarilla, P.O. Box 216, Albuquerque NM 87103.

6.	Certificate of Counseling from an approved credit counseling service.
7.	Copies of all your bills and a list of other amounts you owe to anyone for anything.

If you plan to file for bankruptcy, be prepared to assemble a lot of personal information about all aspects of your finances. You must be completely honest and thorough so that you do not potentially subject yourself to fraud charges. The attorney will walk you through every step of the process.

Item six in Table 9-4 requires a certificate of counseling from an approved credit counseling service. As mentioned at the beginning of this Chapter, all debtors must attend the first class before they file for bankruptcy and a second class before their debt is discharged. The purpose is to provide financial counseling to help debtors avoid putting themselves in this situation again.

Tip 6: List All Assets

During the bankruptcy process, you will be required to list all your assets in addition to your debt. Several schedules will be filed as part of your paperwork. Schedule A requires you to list the following:

- All real property in which you have an interest,
- The nature of your interest,
- Whether the property is owned by the husband, wife, joint or community,
- The current value, and
- The amount of a secured claim.

Such a secured claim is typically a mortgage. You cannot during the bankruptcy process discharge a mortgage and keep the house.

Rather, you can make arrangements to keep paying the mortgage or release the house back to the bank through foreclosure, short sale, deed in lieu of foreclosure, or another mechanism. A bank must take affirmative legal steps to initiate a foreclosure. You may also negotiate to convince a bank that accepting a short sale or deed in lieu of foreclosure would be in its best interest. For a short sale, the bank must approve the selling price. This can delay sales for months, particularly if there is more than one lender involved.

Schedule B requires you to list all personal property, including

- The type of property,
- Its description,
- Whether it is owned by the husband, wife, joint, or community, and
- The current value of the debtor's interest in the property.

The type of property will include (1) cash on hand; (2) checking, savings and other financial accounts; (3) security deposits with public utilities and landlords; (4) household goods, books, pictures and art work; (5) wearing apparel, furs and jewelry; firearms and hobby equipment; and (6) interests in insurance policies, and annuities. The list includes approximately 35 items covering anything that you own that has value. Personal property should be valued at garage sale prices.

On Schedule C, list the property claimed as exempt. This is property that cannot be seized by creditors. Table 9-5 contains examples of some of the exemptions available as of February 12, 2013. These amounts are adjusted every three years. Your lawyer will update you with current numbers, or you can search the internet.

Table 9-5. Federal Bankruptcy Exemptions	
Item	*Exempt Amount*
Homestead	$ 155,675
Maximum aggregate value of assets in individual retirement accounts exempted	$ 1,245,475

The homestead exemption is particularly important for homeowners as it may prevent the forced sale of a home to meet the demand of creditors. Individual retirement accounts are exempt from seizure up to $1,245,475. Consult an attorney for a full list of property that may be exempt under current bankruptcy laws.

On Schedule D, list all creditors holding secured claims. If you have no such creditors, you merely leave the schedule blank. Schedule E requires a listing of all creditors holding priority claims, such as domestic support obligations, contributions to employee benefit plans, taxes and debts owed to governments, and claims for death or personal injury while the debtor was intoxicated. While these are not dischargeable, you should list them if required. If you owe taxes to the IRS, seek to enter into negotiations through their offer and compromise process.

Schedule F is where debtors list creditors holding unsecured non-priority claims. These include credit cards, bank cards, and mail-order house cards. For each debt, the list requires:

- The creditor's name,
- Creditor's address including zip code,
- Creditor's account number, the date the claim was incurred and the amount of claim.

Depending on the number of creditors, this schedule can go on for several pages.

Schedule G requires debtors to list executory contracts (which some courts have defined as "a contract where performance remains due on both sides") and unexpired leases of real or personal property, including timeshare interests. Schedule H is where the person names co-debtors such as a spouse. On Schedule I, debtors list current income while on Schedule J debtors indicate current expenditures, or the person's average monthly budget.

This process is complicated and can overwhelm a debtor in the abstract. The important thing is to breathe, relax, and work through one schedule at a time. Some schedules can be skipped if they do not apply to your circumstances.

Tip 7: During Bankruptcy, Do Not Accept Credit

While you are going through the bankruptcy process, do not take out any more credit. Some unscrupulous companies will offer you loans, knowing that under the rules you will not be able to get rid of the new debt for at least eight years. Also, debts incurred at a time when you know you'll be filing for bankruptcy do not get discharged. After Published Poet filed for bankruptcy with over $50,000 in unpaid credit bills, a car company sent her the letter in Table 9-6 offering to help her finance the purchase of a car or truck. Table 9-6 leaves out the name, address, phone number and other identifying details of the company, but you will get the picture.

Table 9-6. Automobile Offer

Auto Approval Center

Toll Free 888-555-5555 ***Financing Your Future***

Date

Published Poet

Address

Good News! Months before your bankruptcy is discharged, we can help you purchase the dependable car or truck you need. Getting credit after a bankruptcy can sometimes be difficult. We offer flexible automobile financing, to help you start over and rebuild your credit.

Our Flexible Financing Allows For:

* 0% Down Payment.

* Reward Payment Plan—interest rates drop as you make timely payments.

* Credit Building Auto Loans—approval before bankruptcy is discharged.

* Auto loan approvable before your Chapter 7 is discharged.

You don't have to wait a year to get the auto credit you need. As soon as you have your ***Creditors Meeting (341)***, we are able to approve an auto loan for you. You can be driving the vehicle you and your family deserve, sooner than ever imagined.

To take the first step toward building a healthy financial future, call me for more information at 1-888-555-5555.

*Get Pre-Approved (before your bankruptcy is discharged) for an auto loan and received up to a $1,500 discount on the price of your automobile.

Sincerely **Promotional Code**

Manager LHM1

This company does not care that the debtor did not pay other creditors. Notice how it encourages the debtor to seek approval *after* the creditors meeting, when the debtor and his representative will meet to discuss the debt. In small bankruptcies, many creditors will not send a representative. This company seeks to become one of the first post-bankruptcy creditors, gambling that they will get paid but later creditors will not as the debtor returns to old ways.

Some individuals have been known to take on debt in anticipation of bankruptcy. For example, one woman charged approximately $10,000 of wedding expenses on her credit cards, telling her friends that she planned to file for bankruptcy after her nuptials. A credit collector showed up at her wedding. When the minister asked, "Is there anyone who objects to this union?" the collector called the bride a fraud. She complained to friends that the collector was rude. However, she was potentially liable for fraud when she incurred debt that she never intended to repay. This kind of debt is non-dischargeable.

Tip 8: Prepare for Your Bankruptcy Hearing

After filing for bankruptcy, you must attend a second financial counseling session. Show up on time and take notes. The goal is to help you not repeat the bankruptcy process. People sometimes speak emotionally about what led them to this point in their lives. This can be cathartic for the speaker and those listening. At the end of the session, you will receive your second certificate, which your attorney must submit with the final filing documents.

An informal hearing will be scheduled, and you will go before the bankruptcy trustee. In theory, creditors can show up at this meeting and ask questions. In reality, they rarely appear. Answer all of the trustee's questions truthfully. Published Poet was an emotional basket case the day of her hearing and barely able to speak. The judge was sympathetic, probably having encountered many people who similarly responded to the gravity of the occasion.

Do not under any circumstances indicate to the trustee that you think you got away with something, such as saying "I got them suckers!" in reference to your creditors. This could signal you planned to rack up debt and not pay your creditors.

Tip 9: Post-Bankruptcy, Do Not Accept Credit Offers

Even more surprising than the credit offers during bankruptcy are the ones that come post-bankruptcy. One credit card company had lost over $10,000 when Published Poet had her debt discharged in bankruptcy, yet it offered her a new credit card. If you wondered how the credit crisis began, this is partly why. Banks made loans to people with no jobs and no assets who could not repay the loans. They then repackaged the loans to unsuspecting buyers. The banks recouped their money upfront and passed the risk to someone else.

After bankruptcy, you will most likely be offered high interest rate loans. Do not fall for such tactics. Vow, instead, to live debt-free. In our credit-card based society, for example, you will need a card to rent cars, reserve airline tickets and hotels on the internet, or purchase items on eBay, just to name a few. You can address this with debit cards or by acquiring pre-paid credit cards. You put money on these pre-paid cards before using them. Thus when you charge against them, you are spending your own money rather than racking up debt.

The bottom line is to think of credit with the quote, "Fool me once, shame on you; Fool me twice, shame on me." Declaring bankruptcy once is understandable given unexpected and difficult circumstances. If you have declared twice, consider re-evaluating your priorities and values. Published Poet, who declared bankruptcy twice, did this. With the aid of a therapist, she strives to live debt-free. Moreover, it is best not to consider filing for bankruptcy until you reach the point where you can live off cash and vow to do so for a long time into the future.

Tip 10: Accept That Your New Freedom Comes with Damaged Credit Ratings

Bankruptcy is time consuming and emotionally draining. It can take six months to a year of your life to complete. For those whose debt became unmanageable and who became scared to answer the telephone for fear of harassing creditors, it may be worth it. You gain freedom from creditors calling, texting, emailing, and sending letters.

Bankruptcy also comes with distinct disadvantages. It remains on your credit report for 10 years. Potential creditors, landlords, and even employers in some jurisdictions will see that you have gone bankrupt. Should you run for political office, newspapers and other media outlets may ask if you have ever gone bankrupt? As a consequence, you may be judged by others as unworthy for credit, to rent, to be employed, or to run for public office.

Weigh the options, the benefits and the burdens, and then decide if bankruptcy is best for you at this time in your life.

PART 4

Improve Financial Well-Being

CHAPTER 10

Free or Nearly Free

"When I grow up, I'm going to be rich and famous, because then everything will be free," my five-year-old nephew said to me one day out of the blue. I thought this an odd comment until I later had an opportunity to test it.

A few years after the O.J. Simpson trial had made attorney Johnnie Cochran a household name, he visited the University of New Mexico to inaugurate the Cochran Scholarship at the Law School. I had to make arrangements to take him and two students to dinner. He told me he liked Italian food, so I called the best Italian restaurant in Albuquerque around 5:30 p.m. on a Friday night. "I need to make a reservation for 7:00 p.m. this evening," I said to the hostess who answered the phone.

"The earliest I can get you in is at eight-thirty," she said.

"Even if my guest is Johnnie Cochran," I replied.

"*The Johnnie Cochran*?"

"Yeah."

"What time did you say you want to come?"

"Seven o'clock."

"You got it!"

The hostess' eyes widened when she saw him. She immediately seated us. She immediately seated us. An entire plate of free appetizers arrived, served by the Maître D'. We didn't want dessert, but a sampling of desserts arrived anyway. The chef came to our table to ask how we liked the food.

I was relieved when the waitress finally brought the check for the main course. Although Johnnie Cochran paid for the main meal, I felt a tinge of annoyance. I had been patronizing that restaurant for over a decade and had never received free appetizers and desserts. Still, the experience proved my five-year-old nephew possessed a certain amount of wisdom.

The good news, however, is that you do not have to become rich and famous to receive free stuff. Much is available to the ordinary mortal at no cost. This Chapter provides several tips on how to take advantage of the free or nearly free.

Tip 1: Feast on Free Food

It's become a running joke in novels to have characters go to Costco at lunch time when they have run out of cash. Why? Because of the delectable samples of fish, chicken, beef, fruit, nuts, chocolate and other products. Grocery stores do the same thing, particularly on weekends when more people shop. They do this to increase the possibility that you will buy the demonstrated item. But there is no obligation to purchase anything. You can nibble and purchase only the items on your list.

To get people in their doors, chain restaurants frequently advertise free meals. Kentucky Fried Chicken's website was overwhelmed by millions of individuals downloading a free grilled chicken meal coupon after the deal was mentioned on *The Oprah*

Show. I missed the show, but a friend called to pass along the deal. Denny's advertised a free breakfast during the 2009 Super Bowl, and millions of people showed up at restaurants across the United States to dine.

Other places to get free food are receptions. Art galleries sponsor wine and cheese receptions to showcase new artists. They know people can be enticed to step in to view the masterpieces on their walls if offered free food and drink. All you have to do is show up dressed nicely and blend into the crowd as you sample the food.

Look for notices of free public events with receptions to follow on the Internet or in local papers. You'll find plenty of free food at those events, such as public graduations that offer overflowing buffets. There are so many people there that no one will notice an extra person or two with good wishes. Some hotels and bars sponsor happy hours where they provide free food and lower their drink prices. Devour dinner this way. It's polite to order something, but this could be as simple as a soda. Always tip the wait staff with at least a dollar.

Tip 2: Exercise for Free

Some individuals spend hundreds, if not thousands, of dollars a year on a gym membership. Why bother when you can exercise at no cost by walking? This is my favorite form of exercise because I can do it anytime, anywhere. No need to make reservations, or worry that other people will overwhelm the equipment. Put on a pair of shoes, and walk out the door.

Walking has a multitude of advantages. It helps you get in shape and maintain your health. It balances your digestive system, and makes sleep easier by regulating your time clock if you do it early in the morning or in the afternoon. It assists your brain in thinking of creative ideas and solving problems. Because it bears your weight, it helps maintain strong bones. I've even heard walking referred to as "moving meditation" as it calms the nerves.

The destinations are endless. Stride to work, the grocery story, or entertainment facilities. Amble in nature and admire cloud formations. Traverse the foothills of mountains and marvel at wildflowers and rock formations. There are well worn footpaths you can follow or you can create your own trail. These benefits cannot be purchased because they are free. All it takes is a decent pair of sneakers.

Increase the health benefits by adding arm exercises to your morning stroll. Do these by themselves or with weights to work out your arms. Start out by doing old fashioned arm circles in small, medium and large forward and backward rotations while walking. Move your arms to build definition in muscles to rival those of First Lady Michelle Obama, who is highly regarded for her shapely limbs.

Remember the push-up and sit-up that you learned in grade school? You can still do these as an adult. Push-ups are wonderful for building arm muscles. They cushion falls as we age because we catch ourselves before we hit or break anything. Sit-ups strengthen the abdomen and help stave off the beer belly or middle aged paunch. Why spend thousands of dollars on liposuction and a hospital stay when you can sculpt a younger looking body for free?

Consider varying your workouts by renting yoga or Pilates tapes at the library, purchasing inexpensive DVDs, or watching routines on YouTube. Yoga helps you stretch and maintain balance. Practice the routines at home without leaving a comfortable temperature in search of a class. The disadvantage is that you do not have an instructor to correct mistakes.

Get a work-out and save money by doing your own housework and chores. Muscles move and the house gets cleaned to your satisfaction without a drain on your finances. It takes me three to four hours a week to clean my home, and I love the feeling of working with my hands. If you find cleaning laborious, consider breaking up the tasks into 30-minute segments. Set a timer and when the 30 minutes is up, stop.

Many health insurance companies are now including free gym membership as a benefit. They do this because they save money when people remain healthier. In-shape individuals generate fewer requests for doctors and medicines. Those with health challenges should check with doctors before beginning any exercise routine. Similarly, senior and multigenerational centers offer classes and exercise equipment.

No matter how you move, you'll feel and look better. Free exercise is also fun and can be done alone, with a buddy or neighbor, or in a group.

Tip 3: Groom Yourself and Others for Free

Take care of your own hair and manicure your nails for free, or trade with friends and relatives. Look for people with nice cuts who style their own hair. Otherwise, consider going to a beauty or barber school. There, students practice cutting, setting, and coloring hair at little or no cost to the patron. The students are in training and supervised. There's unlikely to be an "uh oh."

Only offer to trade grooming services if you have skills. While I was in graduate school, a student lacking such talent gave the impression that she clipped her hair in the dark. I once volunteered to cut a housemate's hair. I did so using a stainless steel salad bowl to provide the cutting line. Years later, he confessed that he went to the barber the next day. The barber took one look at his head and said, "I hope she was pretty."

These days, I accept that my trimming skills are limited, and only lovingly cut the hair of my brother who is in a coma. Since he never looks in a mirror, I figure he won't mind.

Tip 4: Barter and Exchange Services and Merchandise

Professionals such as dentists, lawyers, masseuses, chefs, and others have exchanged services for years. Farmers barter produce for meat. Parents form babysitting co-ops to swap childcare duties. Some people trade clothing and other items they no longer want for things they currently need. The possibilities are endless.

The trick is to figure out what you are really good at that other people might want. I have traded home cooked gourmet meals, complete with wine, for maintenance help around the house. Through websites, like www.craigslist.com, you can find others willing to swap their skills for yours. Be careful, as such websites have been used by predators seeking victims and accounts can be hacked.

Tip 5: Travel for Free

If you don't mind roughing it, camping is the old fashioned method of traveling and sleeping for free. With a tent and a sleeping bag, you can sleep just about anywhere. If national or state parks are full, check out nearby forests. Truck stops, fitness centers, and swimming pools often have showers available for little or no cost. Photographer Craig Stephenson has asked motels if he can shower in an unmade room. For a $5 tip, he has been given a towel and a bar of soap. You can travel the country on a low budget if you're willing to camp and buy your food at grocery stores.

Pack light to save money. Airlines charge between $20 to $200 per bag, depending on the number of bags and their weight. Consider carrying on small bags for free.

Sleeping on trains is another method that photographer Craig Stephenson uses to save hotel cost. If you are a person who can sleep at an incline, then an overnight trip using public transportation could save you money. Booking tickets during off season increases the possibility of an empty seat next to you.

Most people are familiar with airlines that give miles for flying on their planes and hotels that offer points for staying at their lodging. Some companies double the miles and points if you obtain one of their credit cards. Also consider signing up for email alerts that advertise quick tips on short notice for less expensive flights.

Tip 6: Sleep for Free

Realtors and owners often seek reliable and conscientious people to live in homes that have been on the market for a while to give them a lived-in feeling. Sometimes the homes will be furnished and you just have to keep the home clean. Other times, you provide the furniture. I lived in a colleague's home that had been on the market for a year in Hawai'i. After a month, it sold. I was happy to have an inexpensive space to live, and she was delighted that my presence helped sell her home. If you do not have a personal connection, contact local services in your area. They interview you and inspect your furniture.

Other people promote themselves as house-sitters or dog sitters for owners who are away on vacation or for work. If the sitter takes on chores like watering plants and caring for animals, they may be paid a small remuneration in addition to the opportunity to live for free. Word of mouth builds reputations and leads to recommendations, so responsibly take care of the homes you occupy. This is a great option for those like Lively Law Student seeking to decrease monthly expenses.

Another possibility is to exchange houses with someone. There are several websites that promote trading homes. If you are a home owner, conduct a background check on court websites before letting a stranger occupy your home.

Tip 7: Acquire Free or Nearly Free Medical Care

If you earn below a certain income, you may qualify for free medical care through the Medicaid program or reduced cost for seniors and the disabled through Medicare. Even if you do not meet income guidelines, you may also get free help by becoming a patient of medical, dental, or counseling students. Universities that train students need people with real problems to work on. These students do their best because they are being graded and supervised by a licensed M.D. They want to make this their profession, and know if they do a good enough job, you may want to stick with them and pay them once they set up practice.

Consider participating in medical studies. You may read about a study to test a new drug or treatment on a problem that has irked you. Sign up, obtain the treatment you need, and receive a small payment. Author Judith Schiess Avila received $200 to participate in a study on rosacea (adult acne). She never knew if she received the drug or the placebo, but the condition cleared up and never returned.

Look up your local medical and dental schools and ask if they have a free clinic. You may be surprised at the quality of the care you receive, and best of all it's free or nearly free.

Tip 8: Visit Law School Clinics

Similarly, law schools train their students to become attorneys by having them practice on real problems. While some schools have income limitations, they may waive them if you present an interesting case. One year, I brought a nonprofit's tax issues to the University of New Mexico tax clinic. The nonprofit had not appropriately registered its status for over ten years. The law student worked diligently to bring the nonprofit's registrations up to date. She even helped minimize the fines.

Call a law school clinic near you and inquire as to whether they might be interested in taking your case. These clinics train students on a wide variety of legal issues, from criminal and business to wills and social security. Best of all is the low or no cost. Lawyers are required to give away a certain number of practice hours for free to fulfill state bar *pro bono* requirements. Thus, even an attorney who seems out of your price range may take your case for free.

Tip 9: Listen to Free Concerts

During the summer months, municipalities often offer complimentary concerts in parks, and on plazas and other grand stages. I've seen amazing talent at events on the mall in Washington D.C. and in New York's Central Park, just to name two cities in the United States. I've also attended free concerts in Mexico, Germany, France, and other countries while traveling. The fantastic atmosphere delivers great entertainment on a summer evening. And, of course, the cost can't be beat.

Tip 10: Borrow Books from the Library

Public libraries purchase many of the books that are on the bestsellers' list and books that are profiled in local newspapers.

They also purchase movies and music that rise to the top of various charts. Some libraries even have videogame machines where you can play your favorite videogames.

The ultimate public facility is the Library of Congress, the world's largest library. There's a myth that it has every book ever printed. Rather, it has free access to books and other material through the copyright registration system. To register books, movies, videogames and so forth, individuals and companies have to deposit two copies of the best edition of the work. If an owner does not voluntarily register a desired book, the Library of Congress sends the owner a letter seeking two copies. If the person refuses to comply, the Library of Congress can impose fines of around $250, the equivalent of what it would cost them to purchase and process two copies of the best edition of the book. This system has enabled the Library of Congress to accumulate, according to its website, "a collection of nearly 142 million items [that] includes more than 32 million cataloged books and other print materials in 470 languages; more than 62 million manuscripts; the largest rare book collection in North America; and the world's largest collection of legal materials, films, maps, sheet music and sound recordings." Since the Library of Congress is funded by taxpayer dollars, you can obtain a reader identification card and request its collection for free.

Similarly, you can get a library card at your local library, and use its collection at your leisure. You can check out the books, movies, music and videogames for a significant period of time. As a taxpayer, you pay for these services, and should take advantage of them.

Lest you think you might be hurting authors when you borrow books from the library, think again. I once heard one author complain that her book had been read by over 2,000,000 people while selling only 500,000–600,000 copies. She expressed irritation that she had autographed one copy of her book for nine people. She thought this outrageous.

For every author who complains about book sharing and the availability of books at the libraries, others celebrate the trend. By purchasing books in advance based on the publisher's catalog, libraries can help turn a book into a bestseller. When he was 83 and frail, I drove author Tony Hillerman (known for *A Thief of Time* and other mysteries set on the Navajo reservation) to a First Friday authors' group meeting where he shared a letter from a fan. He had opened this letter and a $100 bill fell out. The fan wrote that she had been checking his books out at the library and realized he might be missing a few royalties. She enclosed a gift.

Over the years, the fan had already given Tony Hillerman the present of increased sales by borrowing his books from the library. When demand increases for a particular authors' book, libraries purchase more copies. It's a win/win situation for all concerned. Take advantage of it.

Tip 11: Cut Back on Cable and Borrow Movies

Similarly, you can eliminate the need for elaborate cable bills by borrowing movies from libraries. Public libraries make available tons of DVDs and Blu-ray films on a first come/first served basis. Often times you can check them out for a week or two. They are free and your only cost is the transportation to pick them up and return them. If you live near a library and can walk or bike there, even better.

Another option is internet television, available through services like Apple TV, T-Mobile TV, or others. You may have to pay for appropriate devices to access these services but they can be a lot less expensive than cable or satellite television services.

Tip 12: Use Computers and the Internet for Free

Another freebie available at libraries is access to their computers. These free computers are available at local public libraries and at university libraries. If you live near a public university, research its libraries. You will find free computers at all of its libraries, including law, engineering and fine arts libraries, just to name a few examples. Simply inquire about how you might use them. Through the web, you can access personal email accounts and save yourself tens of dollars a month.

Further, airports and some retailers offer free internet access. Many Starbucks and Whole Foods, for example, permit wireless access to their websites while in their stores.

Tip 13: Rejoice with Better than Free

When I mentioned the title of this Chapter to photographer Craig Stephenson, he replied, "My favorite is better than free. That's when they pay you." He then rattled off examples like getting paid to drive someone's car to a place you want to go and receiving quadruple the normal interest on checking accounts to use debit cards and maintain a certain balance.

Some retired individuals with time to spare become background extras on television and movie sets. As mentioned in Chapter 8 on Downsizing, retired businessman Scott Lovering earned over $2000 as an extra on a Terminator film. Wily Writer got paid $9 an hour to be an extra in the movie *Sleepless*. For ten hours, she talked to the recent widower seated next to her while waiting for their scene to be shot. She married him five months later.

From ages five to 85, people like receiving free services and things. It's fun and it helps you improve your financial well-being in both healthy and weak economic times.

CHAPTER 11

The Great Life

Currently, many individuals spend too much time overwhelmed by deadlines, choices, demands. Ultimately, we seek to experience the great life, one populated by people we love and work we enjoy. Here are some tips for further enhancing your lifestyle to build a happier and healthier existence.

Tip 1: Less Is More

All the happiness experts are in agreement on one issue: acquiring more stuff does not increase our happiness quotient. All it does is add to our stuff quotient. As mentioned in Chapter 3, most people wear 20% of their clothing 80% of the time. When you consider this, what are you doing with the other 80%? Does it fit? Do you like the colors? When you are about to purchase something, ask yourself will this be part of the 20% worn 80% of the time or part of the 80% worn 20% of the time? While keeping garments for special occasions is to be expected, closets overflowing with rarely or never worn clothing waste space and money. Donate all the clothes you haven't worn in the last two years, especially those in sizes that no longer fit or colors you no longer like. This makes room for the new to come into your life.

The same goes for other items like old computers and other electronic items that have lost their usefulness. If you are not using them, why not donate them? An annual clean-out is a good thing; semi-annual is even better. Annual clean-outs usually work best at the end of the year between December and January or the beginning of the summer between May and June. Both represent times for renewal. If you are ambitious, then do both times.

With winter and spring clean-outs, vow to remove all that you don't use or doesn't give you pleasure. You'll be surprised how good it makes you feel to give items away or discard them at the dump.

Afterwards, when you do buy things, only buy clothes that will be worn and other items that will be utilized. Published Poet adjusted to a life of acquiring fewer items as she balanced her budget and committed to living within her means. You can do this as well and be much happier for it.

Tip 2: Spend More Time with Friends and Family

There are people who cause your energy to soar. You smile when you see them, and the smile remains the entire time you are with them. You laugh hearing their voices on the phone and enjoy their company. You click.

These are the people you want in your life. See them as often as you can. Arrange coffee dates, or to meet at each other's homes. Invite these folks over for tea or lunch, to play games, or to watch special events such as the Super Bowl or the Academy Awards. Hike in a forest with them and stop to smell the tree bark. Ponderosa pines, for example, give off a vanilla scent. Expand a one and a half hour hike into a three-hour stroll as you pause by the river to listen to the spring run-off from melting snow, or to observe trees gently swaying in the wind on a bright sunny day.

Playing financial games, such as *Monopoly* or *CashFlow*, can improve your financial IQ while spending time with family and friends. While *Monopoly* has been around for decades, *CashFlow* is a more recent invention by Robert Kiyosaki, the author of the bestselling book *Rich Dad, Poor Dad*. With *CashFlow*, all participants start out in the Rat Race (sound familiar?) and the aim is to escape onto the Fast Track by buying investments so that your passive income from rentals and businesses exceeds your expenses. It takes two to four hours to play, and participants have fun making choices as opportunities for big and small deals arise.

Just for the fun of it, consider hosting a party at least once a year. This can be to celebrate the usual suspects, such as birthdays, Christmas, Hanukkah, Kwanza, the New Year, St. Patrick's Day, Fourth of July, and Valentine's Day. Also, be open to throwing the unusual, such as an art party to showcase a friend's art or a new recipe party to expose friends to new recipes you've discovered. One colleague who was changing jobs threw a "come drink my wine so I don't have to move it" cocktail party. Sporting events, such as the Super Bowl, the World Series, or the Kentucky Derby, present wonderful opportunities to mingle during intermissions and commercial breaks. The possibilities are endless. Have you had your party this year? If not, start planning. The more you invite others, the more likely you are to receive invitations.

Budget for your party, and throw a great one for $50 to $100. Figure out how many guests, plan the menu, and then go shopping. You can throw in a shrimp tray from Costco or chicken wings from Trader Joe's. Buy the cheese and crackers and create your own tray. A bottle of wine and you're all set. If you can only afford one bottle, make it a red, and buy some fruit and a can of Sprite®,

Sierra Mist®, or similar soda to turn it into Sangria punch, which is always a hit at parties.

Try trading parties with a circle of friends. While living in Hawaii, I joined a military group who rotated hosting Soul Food Sundays. Every Sunday, we would meet at a different person's home. The host would provide the main dish and everyone else would pitch in with a side dish, drinks, or paper products.

Also consider Kamikaze potlucks. With these, a group gets together, and everyone just brings something. It's a food adventure because you never know what you're going to get.

Tip 3: Prepare for Holidays with a Budget and Stick to It

Establish a budget for how much you will spend on recurring events, like major holidays, birthdays, and so forth. Since these events occur annually, you can anticipate their cost. For example, if you know you need to buy Christmas presents for 12 people and you can afford $400, why not buy throughout the year? Spend about $33 every month. Seize sale items that you think a person might like. If you get one person's gift for $15, you can spend more on another individual. When you make your list and stick to your budget, the holidays can be fun. Pay with cash. That way you won't grimace in January and February when the bills come due.

Another tip is to create a gift closet that contains various items acquired throughout the year, preferably on sale. When you are out shopping and see a fun thing that would make a great gift, buy it and add it to the closet. This way the next time you are invited to a birthday or other party and don't have time to shop, you can just pick out a gift from your closet. It's fast.

Having a gift closet makes it easy to give the un-expected gift at an un-expected moment. People love receiving gifts for no reason. Their faces light up into radiant smiles that last throughout the day and sometimes into their week.

Tip 4: Take Vacations

Vacations permit you to recharge your batteries by getting away from your routine. In August, decide where you want to go between now and the next August and start saving. Some banks set up vacation accounts that permit automatic transfers when your paychecks come into the account. The nice thing about automatic transfers is that you don't miss the money. You can track deals on airline tickets, hotels, and car rentals, and then grab the best one.

Even if your finances do not allow getaways, plan to take time off to catch up around the house and yard. Fixing and repairing items will recharge your life and give you loads of energy. It sounds counterintuitive that spending energy cleaning could generate energy, but it does and it increases your pride in your living space.

Tip 5: Accept Life's Challenges and Do Your Best

In some instances we have to be challenged in order to grow. Some trials and tribulations are so severe they devastate you. As mentioned in a previous chapter, the oldest of my brothers has been in a coma since November 2009. He suffered a cardiac arrest while barbequing on the patio of his condo and lost oxygen to the brain for 28 minutes while paramedics worked diligently to revive him. Several doctors stated that he continued to have brain stem function, and thus was not brain dead.

My brother's condition tested me in ways I never expected. I was visiting his town for a conference and on my way to his home the night of the barbeque. I called his cell phone to obtain better directions. A police officer answered and told me my brother had suffered a heart attack. He directed me to the condo and then led me to the hospital. I ended up spending a week sleeping on a cot in my brother's room in the hospital's Intensive Care Unit. I had never been to an ICU before.

While I shed many tears contemplating my brother's demise, several good things came from this experience. I met amazing nurses who were dedicated to their profession and full of empathy toward their patients and family members. The chaplains were generous with their time and supportive as I contemplated what to do about my brother's care. As I told the story to students, colleagues and acquaintances, they reached out to me and offered assistance. I learned from this experience not to keep tragedies bottled up.

No matter how strong you think you are, if there's help available, take it. Be open to the kindness of friends and strangers. You will be amazed at the assistance that comes your way. Two colleagues covered my classes for a week so I could spend time with my brother in the ICU. Another colleague loaned me his car for three months so that I could drive my car to my brother's city and just fly back and forth. A fourth colleague gave me a complimentary Southwest Airlines ticket. A friend of a friend loaned me a condo so I wouldn't have to pay for hotel rooms. The generosity brought tears to my eyes as it comforted my soul. In the midst of a tragedy, friends and strangers contributed to my emotional well-being.

Hopefully, you will never receive a challenge of this magnitude, but if you do realize that you can survive it. All that you can expect of yourself is to do your best. At the same time, you must take care of your own health. If that goes, you will not be of use to those who need your assistance.

The same is true for when family members and friends pass on to the great beyond. Whether a person dies from a long illness or unexpectedly as a judge did when he collapsed while speaking to a law school class, it can throw those who know them for a loop. The closer the person was to you, the more your world order will be disoriented. Take time to grieve. In Elisabeth Kubler-Ross's book *On Death and Dying*, she identifies the five stages of grief as including denial, anger, bargaining, depression, and acceptance. Writing a gratitude letter to the departed where you detail all that you appreciate about them and your relationship can help with accepting the transition.

Tip 6: Cultivate an Attitude of Gratitude

Become grateful for everything and you will be surprised at how many good things you will attract in to your life. Thank your family and friends for being around to support you in good and hard times. Thank supportive parents for giving birth to you. Thank friends who provide lifts when you need them. Be grateful for your spouse, life partner, or intimate companion. Compliment the person on at least one attractive quality on a daily basis.

Always thank people for gifts. Call, email, or handwrite a note. I love receiving such letters in the mail. Since most communication has become digital, handwritten letters are all the more special. In these letters, be sure to mention the specific gift and how you plan to use it.

Be grateful for all the large and small blessings you receive on a regular basis, such as the parking spots that are always there just as you need them or the meter that is full of time when you've run out of coins.

Accept gifts others offer. While *The Bible*, perhaps the world's most quoted book, says "It is more blessed to give than to receive," if you do not graciously receive offers, you hamper the ability of others to give. Receiving and giving balance out in the cycle of life. Cultivating an attitude of gratitude will improve your life immensely.

Tip 7: Practice Random Acts of Kindness

Smile and say hello to people. While this act of kindness is common in small towns, it blows people away in big cities like New York, particularly when you couple it with an unexpected gift. One of my favorite events is Book Expo America because publishers give away free books to attendees to showcase their new publications. I often re-gift books while standing in line at the post office. I'm so shocked at the surprise that appears on people's faces when a stranger gives them something. I've even given away the packaging tape when I've completed bundling up boxes of books. The looks that I get are priceless.

If you live in an area with toll roads, pay the toll of the person behind you. That has happened to me before, and it totally made my day.

When you see someone standing at an intersection requesting money, why not give them something? I was driving novelist Tony Hillerman to a writing event when he spotted a beggar at an intersection, and asked me to hand him a $10 bill. If you do not have or feel comfortable parting with dollars, give a bottle of water or an apple. The person may be hungry or thirsty, and think of the pleasure you will get from giving them food and drink.

Tip 8: Volunteer

Give of your time to local community groups. It can be one hour a week, a month, or a year, but do something. I like to volunteer for a group called CREW, which refurbishes shelters and community centers that support women and children. We meet once a month and give of our labor. One year, we removed industrial glue from a floor that had been previously carpeted. The work was backbreaking, using muscles we didn't know we had, but rewarding.

Volunteering puts a smile on your face. It's good to serve others, whether individuals or groups.

Tip 9: Periodically Unplug Technology

With the proliferation of cell phones and smart phones that permit people to call, text, or send email 24/7, one can feel constantly available. Sometimes it's good to make yourself unavailable, at least part of the day. Julie Morgenstern wrote the book "Never Check E-mail in the Morning" in which she urged people to stop checking email before 11:00 a.m. and then only check it two times after that. The problem with email is that once you open it, you feel obliged to check it all the time and don't get the most important thing of the day done.

Also, don't send email late at night when you're tired and certainly not when you're angry. No matter how urgent it may seem, it's best to wait rather than regret the words. Cyberspace magnifies mistakes, quickly. At a computer company, a woman accidentally sent a love note intended for a married man to a distribution list. One of the recipients forwarded the email to the entire company. As a consequence, she took a hit to her ego.

Then there were the emails, texts, Facebook and Twitter messages that former New York Congressman Anthony Weiner sent to various women. The pictures and words ended up on the Internet for all to see. Before you hit send, pause and ask the following: Can this message survive the scrutiny of daylight? Can I live with having this message being stored in a file for the rest of my life? If you feel compelled to type it, save it and then re-evaluate whether to send it after a goodnight's rest.

Tip 10: Gift Yourself Unstructured Time

Teachers have summers to recuperate. Even if teaching is not your profession, you can give yourself a day, week, or month of unstructured time where you do not have commitments and can do whatever you like, including sleeping or lying in a hammock listening to a waterfall. Unstructured time permits you to go with the flow if something does strike your fancy. You can expand the time of hikes, trips to museums, and dining with family and friends. Time is one of the best gifts to yourself. Award it often.

Tip 11: Have Fun

Ultimately, life is to be enjoyed. You never know when it will come to an end or a sudden pause, like when my brother went into a coma. It gave me great joy to meet my brother's neighbors as I packed up his apartment. They told me how happy he was the day of his barbeque. Better to pause your life on a high note.

One of my best writer friends was Sue Mann, an extraordinary person, who loved having a good time. Sue found kicks on Route 66 and everywhere she walked, hiked, climbed, or drove. At her memorial service, one person said "Sue wouldn't do anything unless it was fun." Another person said, "If it wasn't fun, Sue would make it fun!" Combining the two creates a takeaway from Sue Mann's life: If it isn't fun and you can't make it fun, don't do it unless you absolutely have to.

* * *

Ultimately the great life is a balanced one that incorporates work, relatives, and friends you love. Have fun when you can and spend money in ways that enhance your energy. I hope the tips in this book bring many high notes into your life. Improving your financial well-being can augment your happiness.